Meals in minutes

Marshall Cavendish

Contributors:
Jean Branthwaite
Gail Duff
Valerie Hedgethorne
Stella Henvey
Jan Jefferies

Weights and measures
Both metric and Imperial measures have been
given throughout this book, Imperial figures
appearing in [ ] brackets. These measures are
not exact equivalents so it is essential to follow
one or other system. Never mix the two sets of
figures.

Published by
Marshall Cavendish Books Limited
58 Old Compton Street
London W1V 5PA

© Marshall Cavendish Limited 1985

ISBN 0 85685 717 3

Printed and bound in Italy by New Interlitho SpA.

CONTENTS

HOW TO SAVE TIME

The key to successful quick cooking lies in planning. Planning a week's menus in advance, keeping a well-stocked store cupboard and being aware of what foods cook quickly will save time, energy and money too!

Shopping
Plan your menus to include as much fresh seasonal food as possible. You will get better value for money and will also keep costs to a minimum. Shop in advance, buying non-perishables in reasonable quantities, if you have storage space. The chart on page 5 lists useful standbys with the maximum recommended storage times. Check your store cupboard regularly and keep the ingredients for complete standby meals ready. If you have a freezer or even a big icebox compartment in your refrigerator, keep some food that can be cooked quickly from frozen or can be defrosted quickly.

Always plan ahead so you can shop for semi-perishables, like fresh fruit and meat, just twice a week, if you have a refrigerator to hold them.

Memorize standard quantities to assist you in shopping: how much chicken or what weight of potatoes your family will eat at one meal. Check on the quantities in recipes you intend to make before you shop, so that you don't, for example, buy 225 g [½ lb] cream cheese and then find your recipe demands 350 g [¾ lb].

Saving time
Saving time does not necessarily mean always producing a meal at short notice. Some preparation processes can conveniently be done in advance. Also, by doubling up quantities in some cases, you will be half way to tomorrow's meal without expending any more time.

If guests are invited and you know you will be rushed—a meal before going out to the cinema, for example—consider whether cooking ahead will not do as well as fast cooking. Many puddings that take time to set require very little preparation. Soup can be made ahead and reheated. Stews are as good reheated and sometimes better than newly cooked.

Learn to take your own short cuts and to keep dependence on cans or the freezer for days when your planning has slipped up. In this way, you will save money. Doubling up quantities is the most obvious example. Make twice the quantity of shortcrust: it will keep for a week in a bag in the refrigerator (and for 3 months in a freezer). When you are making a hot rice dish, plan tomorrow's menu round a recipe calling for cold rice. Buy enough meat to provide for more than one meal. Think how you are going to cook the leftovers at the same time as planning the first dish. Look up both recipes and shop for the extra ingredients, such as peppers for stuffing, when you shop for the main dish.

Emergency cooking
Put things by specially for emergencies. Know your recipes and replace those stores when you use them. Remember to turn them over too; they will not keep indefinitely. Keep a few things in reserve for an emergency guest meal and more for family meals. You do not want to end up giving your family exotic canned vegetables because you forgot to replace the canned tomatoes.

It is generally easier, and the best policy for emergency family eating, to put several dishes on the table simultaneously, rather than having a meal of several courses. On the other hand, if you have almost been caught out by visitors and have to feed them in a scramble, putting a first course on the table may well give the main course the time needed to cook and will save a lot of weary waiting around for the meal to begin.

Time-saving equipment
Use oven-to-table ware or a flame-proof casserole when possible. This saves time before the meal and also saves washing up!

If you have a pressure cooker, use it as much as possible and get into the habit of it. Learn what it can cook as well or better than covered cooking and what it does less well. Vegetables, for example, taste better steam-cooked in a pressure cooker than they do boiled. You may find meat will lose its colour if you pressure cook it, but it will be tender very quickly and you can pre-fry it or finish it some other way.

Leave your food mixer and liquidizer, if you own them, where they are easily accessible and near a power point. Then you will use them to speed up a job, without wasting time getting them out.

A freezer is a useful aid to meal planning, but often is no good in a hurry, because you have to wait for food to defrost. In the chart (below) you will find a list of things that can be used from frozen or defrosted in a hurry. Remember always to freeze in small portions to speed defrosting.

QUICK COOKING FROM FROZEN

Soups and sauces: reheat in pan over low heat

Fish: can be fried, poached or baked from frozen

Liver: can be fried from frozen; allow 20 minutes

Chops, lamb or pork: can be grilled from frozen, allow 30 minutes

Small meat balls: fry from frozen in 6 mm [¼"] fat or reheat in sauce

Stews or casseroles for one or two: can be reheated from frozen if portions are small

Vegetables: many at their best from frozen

Bread: sliced bread can be toasted from frozen

Cake: small sponge cakes and slices packed between paper defrost in very little time

Baked flan cases: defrost in moderate oven for 10 minutes

Planning balanced meals
When cooking fast meals, more often than not all thought of nutrition goes by the wayside. One such meal

now and again does no harm. A diet based on convenience food, often giving prominence to frying as a cooking method and carbohydrates as ingredients, can well make you undernourished and overweight simultaneously: proper planning is essential.

Most cooks find it convenient to plan round the protein of the main course necessary for body building and repair. Unfortunately, the quick protein food—steak and chops—are also the most expensive. It is possible, however, as the recipes show, to plan round the cheaper protein foods and to compensate by including milk, eggs, cheese or pulses if the meal is light on meat or fish.

Include a variety of vegetables, salads or fruit throughout the week to include vital vitamins and minerals. Salads are the fast cook's friend, as the recipes show, you need not be in any way boring or repetitive. If you stick firmly to seasonal vegetables—and include fruit in them too —they need not be expensive even in winter.

Cook your vegetables correctly. Do not soak green vegetables. Fortunately it is easy to avoid overcooking them if you are in a hurry. A bowl of fruit to conclude the meal is good for you and a quick dessert.

Carbohydrates—the starches and sugars—are the cheapest form of food stuff and often the quickest. Avoid relying on them too much when in a hurry. Sugar provides energy, but if more is eaten than is needed, it will provide you with extra round the waistline too. In particular, try to make it a rule not to provide sweet snacks when time is too short for a proper meal: make them savoury ones. The other carbohydrates do at least give some vitamins and minerals. Bread, for example, has a little protein as well as vitamin B and calcium.

Fats are needed for heat and energy, but it is best not to over indulge. This can cause indigestion and again will make you fat and unhealthy. In particular, avoid relying on frying too much.

Making meals attractive

Well planned meals should be attractive as well as nutritious. Do not attempt a dish that you have not got time to complete properly. It is better to cook something more simple and eat it at its best! Try to avoid the same method of cooking throughout a meal. It makes a meal much more interesting and also more nutritionally sound if the methods of cooking are varied. For example, it is better to serve fried fish and chips followed by poached fruit, rather than pancakes; or steak and kidney pudding followed by fresh fruit salad, rather than syrup pudding.

Texture and colour also play important parts. Even in the same course, different textures should be provided, some creamy and some crunchy, some dry and some moist. This also makes for ease of eating. All sloppy foods on a plate are difficult to manage, as are all very dry ones.

Dishes of a similar colour can look boring and unappetizing. Try to have some colour which harmonizes or contrasts, either in the form of a vegetable accompaniment or a decoration. It will immediately make the meal more inviting. It often only needs a few peas, a slice of lemon or tomato wedge. Even when you are in a hurry these touches are worthwhile.

Choose flavours which complement each other and bring out the virtues of the food. The same flavour, food or decoration, however, should not be used twice in a meal. For example, do not serve tomato soup followed with grilled tomatoes as a vegetable, or risotto followed by a rice pudding.

Roger Phillips

Store-cupboard sense

A well-stocked store cupboard serves several distinct purposes. In it you will keep the household basics like pasta, rice and flour, from which you can conjure up quick meals (see handy hints box). With your spices and flavourings you have the means to turn the plain staples from the refrigerator or the vegetable rack into more interesting meals; by adding herbs to an omelette, for example, or by making a spicy brown sauce for sausages or bacon.

You will also want cans of things like tuna, sardines in oil or tomato sauce, anchovies and sweetcorn kernels because they are inexpensive, popular and you are unlikely to be able to buy them fresh. Other things like canned tomatoes are as good as, but cheaper, than the fresh ones.

There are also the more luxurious items such as canned peaches and pineapples which lend variety to a dull winter diet. You may also have a small store of more exotic vegetables or fruit on which you can rely when guests appear at meal times with very little or no notice.

Convenience food, from cake mixes to cook-in sauces or canned suppers, always saves time but you will often sacrifice both quality and money. Some convenience foods like custard powder and gravy browning find their way to most homes. Before buying any convenience food, consider exactly what you are saving. It is hardly worth buying canned spaghetti or rice in any form, because both are quick and easy to cook. If you find cook-in sauces helpful, remember that with canned tomatoes, appropriate herbs and a little vinegar in the cupboard, you could well be minutes away from your own, fresh-tasting cook-in sauce.

However, if your family has a taste for boiled suet puddings or for rice pud, you may find it worth buying these from time to time. Because of the long cooking period involved and the expense in fuel this may be their only chance of eating such things!

If you do not have even a small freezer, then you will probably need a small stock of canned protein—from mince to frankfurters. Shop around until you find brands that your family likes and that gives you value for money—stew with plenty of meat chunks, for instance, and not all the gravy that you could make yourself.

The chart lists things that a well-stocked store cupboard should contain and gives recommended storage times. It is unlikely that food will come to harm if kept a little longer than these times, but try to eat them earlier, as both flavour and texture will deteriorate.

Safe storage

This is essential for health and economy. There is little point in buying and storing food if it has to be thrown away because it has deteriorated beyond the point when it can be eaten. (The storage chart on page 5 tells you how long to keep food.)

Most canned and packaged goods should be kept at a constant temperature which is cool and dry, rather than hot and humid. Ideally, they should be stored in kitchen cupboards or shelves that are as far as possible away from the oven and any direct source of heat, such as central heating and hot water pipes.

Be careful that you do not buy dented, rusted or stained cans. Avoid also those which are 'blown' (top and bottom curve outwards rather

Handy hints
Quick-cooking foods for the store cupboard
rice: 12–15 minutes
pasta: 10–15 minutes
small dumplings: 20 minutes
pancakes: 3–4 minutes each

Handy hint

Storing canned hams
Be careful when storing canned hams. Pasteurized ham weighing less than 1 kg [2 lb 3 oz] can be stored for up to 6 months in a cool cupboard, as can a small sterilized ham. A sterilized ham over 1 kg [2 lb 3 oz] should always be stored in the refrigerator and for no longer than 6 weeks. Before buying a canned ham, therefore, check carefully to see whether it is sterilized or pasteurized and choose the ham according to when you plan to eat it.

Roger Phillips

than being flat). If a chemical change has taken place inside the can, consuming the contents can be very dangerous. Remember to rotate your canned and packaged food so you use the oldest first. You might find it useful to mark the date and year of purchase on your containers and cans with indelible pencil. Do not forget to wash your shelves down regularly as well.

Once opened, dry goods are best kept in suitable containers. Use screw top jars, plastic containers, or tins. Make sure that the containers are completely clean and dry before using. When re-filling, always empty, wash, dry and then re-fill with the new stock. Never put new on top of old. Label everything clearly, especially white powders which look alike.

If you have the space, you might find it useful to have a reserve shelf containing foods that can be combined for an emergency meal and also items used only for special occasions. When anything is taken from the shelf, make sure it is replaced as soon as possible.

The refrigerator
The refrigerator is a cold storage cupboard where perishables can be kept briefly at 5°C [40°F]. In the chart you will find things that ought always to be kept there; fix in your mind the recommended storage times and try to ensure a regular turnover. Fresh foods which are usually bought for specific meals, rather than for general use, are covered in the following few pages.

USEFUL FOOD FOR STORING

	maximum storage time
Canned foods	
Condensed soups	2 years
Evaporated and condensed milk	9 months
Fish in oil: tuna, sardines, mackerel	5 years
in tomato sauce	1 year
Fruit: peaches, pears, pineapple	1–2 years
prunes and rhubarb	1 year
Meat: corned beef, luncheon meat, meat balls,	
mince, stewed steak	5 years
Milk puddings	1 year
Vegetables: baked beans, beansprouts, carrots,	
celery hearts, peas, potatoes, sweetcorn, tomato	2 years
Dry foods	
Arrowroot	6 months
Baking powder	6 months
Bicarbonate of soda	6 months
Biscuits	3 months
Cocoa	6 months
Coffee: instant and ground, sealed in a tin	1 year
Cornflour	6 months
Cream of tartar	3 months
Custard powder	6 months
Dried fruit: currants, sultanas, glacé cherries,	
angelica	6 months
Dried milk	6 months
Drinking chocolate	6 months
Flavourings: salt, white and black pepper, mustard,	
stock cubes or powder, vanilla and almond essences	1 year
Flour	6 months
Golden syrup, treacle	1 year
Herbs and spices: mixed herbs, oregano, bay	
leaves, garlic granules, curry powder, cinnamon,	
mixed spiced, nutmeg	9 months
Nuts: almonds, walnuts	2 months
Pasta: macaroni, shells, spaghetti, tagliatelle	1 year
Pulses: dried peas and beans, lentils	1 year
Rice: long and short grain	1 year
Sugar: caster, granulated	5 years
icing	1 year
Tea	2 weeks or less
Preserves and bottled goods	
Jams, mincemeat, marmalade	1 year
Mayonnaise/salad cream	1 year
Oil: try to keep a selection of oils eg:	store in cool,
olive oil, a good quality salad oil and	dark place, up
a general purpose cooking oil	to 6 months
Pickles and chutneys	1 year
Tomato purée	6 months
Tomato sauce	6 months
Vinegar: try to keep a selection eg:	
malt, white wine, tarragon	2 years
Refrigerated food	
Bacon	1 week
Butter, salted and unsalted	up to 1 month
Cheese: Cheddar, Edam etc	1–2 weeks
Eggs, fresh	2 weeks
Lard	1 month
Margarine	2 months
Milk	3 days

Quick-cook fresh food

Convenience foods may be easy to buy, but they will often take as long as fresh foods to actually cook. Fresh seasonal food is the proper basis for any menu planning; happily many types do not take long to prepare and cook quite quickly. The fastest prepared foods are outlined here, with the best methods for fast cooking.

MEAT

The better and more expensive cuts are best for quick cooking as they contain less muscles and connective tissue. 'Tough' cuts demand long, slow cooking to soften them; never attempt to do these by a quick-cooking method.

Pork

Most pork can be cooked quickly, although it is important to cook it thoroughly. Grilling and frying are the fastest methods, but some short-time casseroles are possible if you use better cuts and fry them first.
● Loin chops: grill for 10–15 minutes on each side according to thickness.
● Spare rib chops: grill in the same way as loin chops, or fry briefly on both sides and then cook in a heated oven with a sauce.
● Shoulder: can be cubed and used with other ingredients for a casserole with sauce.
● Belly (streaky rashers): is good grilled or casseroled.
● Fillet: cut into slices and grill or fry.

Beef

The fast-cooking cuts are the most expensive ones and this makes them suitable only for the more special occasions.
● Steak: fillet is the most expensive, it needs very little cooking. Grilling is best and takes only a few minutes each side, depending on how you like your steaks. Fresh fillet can be minced raw and mixed with egg yolk and chopped vegetables and herbs to make classic 'steak tartare'.
● Rump and porterhouse: take a few minutes longer than fillet because it is best to lower the heat after the initial sealing.
● Cheaper steaks: must be cooked more slowly, even when labelled 'frying steak'.
● Mince: can be cooked in 20–30 minutes.

Veal

Cuts of veal without muscle are very quick cooking. The meat is dry and without fat, so frying is best, especially when the veal is coated with egg and crumbs first.
● Fillet or escalopes: need only a few minutes frying on either side.
● Cutlets: best coated and fried.

Lamb

Choose tender cuts without muscle.
● Chump or loin chops: grill or fry for about 7 minutes on each side.
● Best end cutlets: better if coated with egg and crumbs and fried.
● Cubed, boned shoulder: can be grilled as kebabs or fried and finished as a quick casserole.

OFFAL

Very quick, nutritious meals can be made from offal; offal has the advantage of being both fast and cheap.

Liver

Choose lambs', calves' or pigs' liver. Ox liver needs long, slow cooking. Although liver can be grilled it is best fried. Do not over-cook it: 5 minutes on either side is enough for calves' and lambs' liver.

Kidneys

Kidneys cook in a matter of minutes. Choose lambs' or pigs' kidneys.
● Lambs' kidneys can be grilled as part of a mixed grill or as kebabs. They are excellent cooked in wine.
● Pigs' kidneys have a stronger flavour. They are best used in sauté dishes and finished with a sauce.

Sausages

Sausages can be grilled or fried, but remember there are boiling sausages which cook in 20 minutes.

CHICKEN

This popular meat cooks quickly when jointed.
● Grilling: a quarter of a small chicken will take 15 minutes grilled on the inside and then a further 10 minutes grilled on the skin side.
● Deep-fat frying is better for larger joints with a bone, because the heat penetrates all round at the same rate. The joints must be coated first.
● Shallow frying is more suitable for small pieces of flat, boneless joints such as breast. Serve accompanied by a sauce.

FISH

All fish cooks quickly. It is a boon to the cook in a hurry because it can be prepared and cooked in a very short time. For freezer owners, it has the additional advantage that it can be cooked without defrosting.
● Cooking times depend upon the type of fish and whether whole, in cutlets or filleted, and will vary from 10–45 minutes. Nearly all methods of cooking are both suitable and fast.
● Grilling: a few minutes on each side, depending on the fish.
● Frying: in deep fat, coated with batter or egg and breadcrumbs; in shallow fat, coated or uncoated.
● Steaming: between 2 plates over a pan of boiling water.
● Poaching: in a small amount of

liquid, such as milk or court bouillon made with fish stock and wine.
● Baking: very useful if you are using the oven to cook something else. A cutlet of fish such as cod will only take 20 minutes to cook.
● Shellfish: bought ready-cooked, this only needs heating through.

DAIRY PRODUCTS
Eggs
Cooking methods such as boiling, poaching, scrambling, frying, baking and omelettes demand only minutes. Soufflés cook in half an hour, once prepared.

Cheese
Cheese in itself needs no cooking to be edible, but it is often added to many dishes—as the main part of the dish, or for extra flavour or food value.
● Au gratin: sprinkled on top before grilling.
● Incorporated into mixtures such as quiches, over and in potatoes, in sauces, etc.
● Fried or toasted sandwiches.

Milk
Milk also needs no cooking, but is often an important ingredient in many recipes, for example, custards and sauces.

VEGETABLES
Vegetables usually take very little actual cooking time: more is spent in preparation. A great deal depends on their age: young ones cook faster.

Green vegetables
Cook leafy vegetables in the minimum of water to conserve food value. Always put them into boiling water.
● Brussels sprouts: take 8 minutes if they are prepared by cutting a cross through the stalk at the bottom (the thickest part).
● Shredded cabbage takes 10–20 minutes.
● Cauliflower: 8–10 minutes if divided into florets before cooking, 20–30 if cooked whole.
● Spinach takes 8–10 minutes if washed then cooked, covered, with only a good knob of butter. The water clinging to the leaves provides all the moisture needed. Stir regularly to prevent sticking.

Root vegetables
● For really quick cooking, slice or grate, then cook in the absolute minimum of water. Purée with the cooking water to retain nutrients. (This makes an excellent base for soup.)
● Try also purées of swede or parsnip instead of potato with your bangers! Dry the purée by returning it to the saucepan and stirring over a low heat to evaporate moisture before adding butter and seasoning.
● New potatoes are best if boiled in their skins—simply wash and scrub clean. Diners can remove skins if wished.

Frozen vegetables
A boon to the busy cook, frozen vegetables provide a choice of out-of-season vegetables and require none of the usual cleaning, etc.

Because they are blanched before freezing, frozen vegetables are quicker to cook than their fresh counterparts. They are also best cooked straight from frozen, so they can be added to a dish at the last minute without previous planning.
● Quickly cooked in boiling, salted water, they are even better when they are braised. Add only about 50 ml [2 fl oz] water per 450 g [1 lb] vegetables as the water from the thawing vegetables will provide sufficient liquid.

Braised vegetables
Some vegetables such as carrots, parsnips and leeks benefit particularly from braising. It is quicker than boiling whole, more interesting to eat and preserves the nutrients lost when boiling sliced vegetables. To braise, turn the sliced vegetable in a knob of butter, margarine or bacon fat, melted, in the bottom of a pan. Add water, stock, wine, tomato juice, milk or other liquid to almost cover. Put on the lid and leave to simmer. The vegetable is ready when the liquid has almost evaporated

Grilled vegetables
● Tomatoes take 5 minutes halved (they can also be baked quickly—about 15 minutes in a hot oven).
● Flat cap mushrooms grill quickly. Dot well with butter.

Sautéed vegetables
● Peel and par-boil root vegetables such as potatoes, parsnips, swedes and turnips. Drain, dry, then cut into wafer-thin slices. Heat enough fat in a sauté pan to cover the base to a depth of 6 mm [¼″]. Cook the sliced vegetables in batches, frying only as many slices as the pan will hold in a single layer at one time. Cook over medium heat for a few seconds on both sides. Continue cooking, shaking the pan to prevent sticking, for 5–10 minutes until golden brown. Drain on kitchen paper.
● Cleaned and sliced chopped celery, fennel, courgettes, onions, leeks and mushrooms can be sautéed without any preliminary cooking.

Salads
Requiring only washing and drying, fresh salad stuffs are the busy cook's greatest ally. If there is time, put them in a plastic bag after washing and return them to the refrigerator so they will become crisp.

Alan Duns

SOUPS AND STARTERS

Soups and appetizers are the easiest of all fast foods as so many of the basic ingredients can be kept in the store cupboard.

Canned fish is excellent for hors d'oeuvres, and with the choice of shrimps, prawns, anchovies, sardines, crab and salmon, it is easy to provide different and interesting dishes.

Frozen vegetables make excellent soup—and this cuts down on the preparation time. Keep a stock of frozen peas and carrots—these are the most useful. Canned tomatoes are good for soup too—especially for the instant gazpacho given in this chapter.

Canned fish ideas
All these starters serve four unless otherwise stated.
Tuna
● For tonno e fagioli, drain a 200 g [7 oz] can of tuna fish. Mix with 400 g [14 oz] drained canned haricot or kidney beans, thinly sliced onion rings and a good French dressing. Garnish with plenty of freshly chopped parsley.

● For tuna pâté, mix 90 g [3½ oz] tuna with 15 ml [1 tablespoon] lemon juice. Add 15 ml [1 tablespoon] finely chopped onion and enough mayonnaise to make a smooth paste—about 75 ml [5 tablespoons]. Use as a spread for toast or as a filling for 4 hard-boiled eggs or 4 tomatoes. Thinned down with more mayonnaise, this pâté makes a good tuna sauce to serve with cold veal or chicken.

● For tuna stuffed tomatoes, hollow out large tomatoes. Fill with 90 g [3½ oz] tuna drained, flaked and tossed with 15 ml [1 tablespoon] each of roughly chopped onion, chopped parsley and lemon juice.

Crab
● Toss 90 g [3½ oz] crab meat with 2 thinly sliced tomatoes, a peeled, stoned and cubed avocado, 2 quartered hard-boiled eggs and 75 ml [5 tablespoons] mayonnaise.

● For crab cocktail, shred crisp lettuce leaves and arrange in the bottom of a glass dish. Stir 190 g [6½ oz] crab meat into 150 ml [¼ pt] mayonnaise coloured pink with 5 ml [1 teaspoon] tomato purée and spiced with a little Tabasco sauce. Pile on to the shredded lettuce. Serves two.

Sardines
● Drain a 200 g [7 oz] can of sardines in oil. Mash thoroughly and season to taste with salt and black pepper. Serve on buttered fingers of toast decorated with a curl of lemon and freshly chopped parsley.

● For sardine pâté, mash 200 g [7 oz] drained sardines with 30 ml [2 tablespoons] lemon juice. Add enough mayonnaise to make a smooth paste—about 60 ml [4 tablespoons]. Stir in 10 ml [2 teaspoons] finely chopped onion and a little curry paste to taste.

Salmon
● For a high speed salmon mousse drain 200 g [7 oz] canned salmon and combine with 150 ml [¼ pt] mayonnaise. Soak 15 g [½ oz] gelatine in

Lettuce and onion soup makes a creamy starter to a meal.

Frederick Mancini

45 ml [3 tablespoons] water, then dissolve over low heat. Cool a moment then stir into the salmon mixture. Whisk 2 small egg whites until stiff then fold into the salmon. Chill in the freezer or freezer box of your refrigerator for 15 minutes to set.

Canned vegetables
Better quality canned vegetables are excellent tossed in a well-flavoured vinaigrette dressing, soured cream or mayonnaise. Good choices are artichoke hearts, asparagus spears, baby beets, button mushrooms, lima beans, haricots verts and blancs and pimentoes.

Instant gazpacho

You will need a freezer or large freezer box on your refrigerator in order to chill this soup quickly.

SERVES 4–6
⧗10 minutes plus
  15 minutes to chill
2 × 225 g [½ lb] canned
  tomatoes
1 large onion
7.5 cm [3″] piece of cucumber
half a green pepper
3 garlic cloves
2 slices of white bread
30 ml [2 tablespoons] olive oil
30 ml [2 tablespoons] white
  wine vinegar
575 ml [1 pt] tomato juice

1 Empty the canned tomatoes into a blender. Peel and chop the onion and add. Chop the cucumber and green pepper and add.

2 Peel and roughly chop the garlic and add. Blend thoroughly.

3 Tear the bread into small pieces and add with the oil and wine vinegar. Blend thoroughly and stir in the tomato juice.

4 Chill for at least 15 minutes.

Lettuce and onion soup

Lettuce makes a delicately flavoured, pale green soup in minutes.

SERVES 4
⧗20 minutes
50 g [2 oz] butter
1 large round lettuce, washed

1 large onion
salt
freshly ground black pepper
575 ml [1 pt] chicken stock
150 ml [¼ pt] thick cream
freshly chopped chives to
  garnish

1 Melt the butter in a heavy-based saucepan over a low heat. Tear the lettuce into pieces, add to the pan and sauté for 3 minutes.

2 Peel and chop the onion. Add to the pan and sauté for 1 minute. Add the seasoning and stock.

3 Simmer for 5 minutes. Purée in a blender. Return to the pan.

4 Stir in cream, re-heat gently. Do not to boil. Garnish with chives.

Cream of avocado soup

A blend of avocado and chicken stock provides an unusual and satisfying soup.

SERVES 4
⧗35–40 minutes
1 large avocado pear
juice of 1 lemon
1 medium-sized onion
40 g [1½ oz] butter
25 g [1 oz] flour
575 ml [1 pt] chicken stock
salt
freshly ground black pepper
75 ml [3 fl oz] thin cream or
  top of the milk

1 Peel the skin from the avocado and remove the stone. Cut the flesh into small cubes and toss in the lemon juice.

2 Peel and chop the onion. Melt the butter in a large saucepan and add the onion. Stir over a low heat for about 10 minutes until soft but not brown.

3 Remove from heat and stir in the flour. Return to the heat and cook for 2–3 minutes.

4 Off the heat, blend in the stock. Return to the heat, bring to the boil and add the avocado cubes. Simmer, covered, for 10–15 minutes.

5 Season to taste then purée in an electric blender or put through a sieve.

6 Just before serving stir in the thin cream or top of the milk.

Spring pea soup

Combined with mint and cream, frozen peas make a quick, elegant soup that can be served hot or cold.

SERVES 4
⧗20 minutes
450 g [1 lb] frozen peas
1 small onion
sprig of mint
50 g [2 oz] butter
575 ml [1 pt] chicken stock
salt
freshly ground black pepper
150 ml [¼ pt] thick cream
mint leaves to garnish

1 Put the peas in a saucepan. Peel and chop the onion and add to the pan. Add the sprig of mint and the butter.

2 Set over a low heat. Stir until peas and onions are coated in butter.

3 Add the stock. Simmer for 10 minutes.

4 Purée in a blender. Return to the pan. Check seasoning. Stir in the cream and re-heat gently if serving hot. Serve garnished with mint leaves.

Parmesan tomatoes

Served piping hot, Parmesan tomatoes make a welcome starter.

SERVES 4
⧗20 minutes
4 large ripe tomatoes
50 g [2 oz] grated Parmesan cheese
salt
freshly ground black pepper
pinch of dried basil
150 ml [¼ pt] thick cream

1 Heat the oven to 190°C [375°F] gas mark 5.

2 Pour boiling water over the tomatoes and let them stand for 1 minute. Drain and cool under cold running water. Nick skin near stalk with a sharp, pointed knife and gently pull away skin. Next, halve and de-seed the tomatoes. Arrange in a flameproof dish.

3 Sprinkle with the cheese, seasonings and herbs.

4 Pour over the thick cream. Cook in centre of the oven for 15 minutes.

Artichoke hearts au gratin

Canned artichoke hearts are used to make this substantial starter. As a first course, it will serve six. As a main course for a supper or lunch, it will serve four.

SERVES 6
⧗20 minutes
400 g [14 oz] canned artichoke hearts in brine
25 g [1 oz] butter
25 g [1 oz] flour
salt
freshly ground black pepper
pinch of nutmeg
425 ml [¾ pt] milk
50 g [2 oz] grated Parmesan cheese
2 slices cooked ham, chopped

1 Drain and dry artichoke hearts; arrange in the base of a large, shallow flameproof dish.

2 Melt the butter in a heavy-based pan over a low heat. Off the heat, stir in the flour, salt, pepper and nutmeg. Return to heat and cook for 2 minutes.

Frederick Mancini

3 Off the heat, stir in the milk. Then bring to the boil, stirring slowly.

4 Off the heat, stir in the cheese. Return to heat and cook gently for 5 minutes.

5 Sprinkle the pieces of ham over artichoke hearts. Pour over the sauce and brown under a hot grill for 5 minutes.

Pear and Stilton salad

You must have very ripe pears for this dish as the fruit is not cooked before serving. The pears can also be served half per person on a bed of dressed watercress.

SERVES 4
⧗10 minutes
4 large ripe pears
45 ml [3 tablespoons] vinaigrette
100 g [¼ lb] Stilton cheese
30 ml [2 tablespoons] thick cream
30 ml [2 tablespoons] brandy
50 g [2 oz] chopped walnuts

1 Cut the pears in half and hollow out the cores by turning a spoon round in the centre. Peel. Toss the pears in the vinaigrette, then drain.

2 Cream the cheese with the cream and brandy to make a smooth paste.

3 Divide the mixture between the pears, piling into the centre cavity and spreading it out to the edges.

4 Stick the pear halves together. Decorate the edges, where you can see the cheese, with chopped walnuts.

Kipper pâté

Boil-in-the-bag kipper fillets take no time to cook and prepare. While the fish is cooking, you can prepare the lemon shells that give this high-speed dish the look of loving care.

SERVES 4
⧗20 minutes plus 10 minutes to chill
225 g [½ lb] boil-in-the-bag kipper fillets
4 lemons
1 garlic clove
75 g [3 oz] butter

1 Cook the fish following the manufacturer's instructions.

2 Meanwhile, cut a thin slice off the base of each lemon so that the fruit will stand upright. Cut off the pointed end to make a lid and reserve.

3 Cut round the inside with a grapefruit knife to scrape the inside of the lemons clean of flesh and segments. Press all the lemon flesh through a sieve and set aside the juice.

4 Turn the cooked fish into a blender. Peel and chop the garlic. Melt the butter and add with the lemon juice and garlic.

5 Blend until smooth. Pile into the lemon shells. Top each with a lid Chill for at least 10 minutes in the freezer or freezer box of your refrigerator before serving.

Quick liver pâté

Pâté takes time to make but using bought liver sausage, you can serve this delicious pâté in minutes. Serve with Melba toast. Alternatively, arrange fingers of fresh carrot, cauliflower sprigs, crisps, olives and other cocktail nibbles on a large flat dish in a wheel pattern, put the pâté in a small bowl in the centre and serve as a dip.

SERVES 4
⧗ 10 minutes
350 g [¾ lb] liver sausage
15 ml [1 tablespoon] brandy or
   dry sherry
50 g [2 oz] butter
pinch of mace
45 ml [3 tablespoons] thick
   cream

1 Remove the liver sausage from its skin and put in a bowl with the brandy or sherry.

2 Beat the butter to soften it, then cream together with the liver sausage and mace.

3 Stir in the cream, adding just enough to make a creamy, but not sloppy, mixture.

Parmesan tomatoes and kipper pâté.

Potted chicken

Left-over chicken can be turned into this appetizer in minutes. Serve with thin slices of toast or with crisp water biscuits.

SERVES 4
⧗ 5 minutes plus
   5 minutes to chill
100 g [¼ lb] cold chicken
75 g [3 oz] cooked ham
salt
freshly ground black pepper
pinch of mace
75 g [3 oz] butter

1 Mince the chicken and ham together, using the fine blade of the mincer.

2 Season to taste. Soften 50 g [2 oz] of the butter and work into the meat mixture to make a smooth paste.

3 Press into ramekins or a small dish. Melt the remaining butter and pour it over the top. Leave in the freezer or freezer box of your refrigerator for 5 minutes to set.

Buttered crab

Traditionally fresh crab is used for this dish, but canned crab works well.

SERVES 4
⧗ 15 minutes
200 g [7 oz] can crab meat
2 anchovy fillets
45 ml [3 tablespoons] dry
   white wine
200 ml [7 fl oz] milk
75 g [3 oz] white breadcrumbs
pinch of grated nutmeg
salt
freshly grated black pepper
50 g [2 oz] butter
4 slices of toast

1 Mash the anchovy fillets and mix with the wine and milk.

2 Add breadcrumbs and season. Boil, then simmer 5 minutes.

3 Drain, then flake the crab meat. Dice the butter and add. Add to the hot wine mixture. Cook for 4 minutes and serve on toast.

Alan Duns

SIMPLE SNACKS

For a light lunch, a late-night bite or a mid-morning breakfast, a savoury snack is the perfect food.

It is in snack cookery that fast foods such as cheese, bacon, eggs and canned fish come into their own. Prepared with imagination (as in the recipes featured in this chapter), cheese on toast can be just as exciting and sustaining as a larger meal.

One thing snacks must not be is junk food, such as sweets, cakes and other 'empty' Calorie carriers. These will not do you any good at all—and the chances are you will still be hungry after that chocolate bar or piece of cake you grabbed because you were in a hurry.

Most of the snacks given in this chapter take only minutes to prepare and all are made from easily available ingredients.

Chicken liver croustades

Chicken livers are always cheap and cook very quickly.

SERVES 4
⏳15 minutes
4 slices of bread
100 g [¼ lb] chicken livers
25 g [1 oz] butter
50 g [2 oz] button mushrooms
salt
freshly ground black pepper
15 ml [1 tablespoon] medium sherry
parsley or watercress to garnish

Frederick Mancini

1 Cut the crusts off the bread and set the bread aside. Wipe and cut any greenish parts off the livers.

2 Melt the butter in a heavy-based frying-pan. Add the livers. Wipe, slice and add the mushrooms. Simmer for 10 minutes. Season to taste.

3 Stir in the sherry. Toast the bread and spoon the mixture on top. Garnish and serve immediately.

Soft roe savoury

Soft roes are cheap when in season or can be bought canned at other times of the year. Soft roes on toast is traditionally an after-dinner savoury but is just as good served as a light supper dish.

SERVES 4
⏳12–15 minutes
12 soft herring roes
50 g [2 oz] butter
4 slices of white bread
squeeze of lemon juice
freshly chopped parsley to garnish

1 Wash and dry the roes. Remove any black or silver threads. Melt half the butter in a heavy-based frying-pan. Fry the roes for 8 minutes.

2 Remove with a slotted spoon and keep warm.

3 Add the remaining butter. Fry the bread on both sides. Spoon roes and buttery juices over the bread. Squeeze a little lemon juice over each serving and top with freshly chopped parsley.

Danish pizza

This is much quicker to make than traditional pizza. The dough base can be used with any topping.

SERVES 2–3
⏳45 minutes
For the topping:
50 g [2 oz] Mozzarella cheese
4 streaky bacon rashers
1 small onion
25 g [1 oz] butter
225 g [½ lb] canned tomatoes
2.5 ml [½ teaspoon] dried oregano
salt
freshly ground black pepper
freshly chopped parsley to garnish

For the dough:
100 g [¼ lb] self-raising flour
2.5 ml [½ teaspoon] salt
50 g [2 oz] melted butter

1 Cut the cheese into strips. Remove rind from the bacon. Fry the rashers in the bottom of a large saucepan until crisp, then set aside.

2 Peel and chop the onion, and add to the pan with the butter. When the onion is soft, add the tomatoes and herbs. Season to taste. Simmer for 2 minutes.

3 For the dough, sift the flour and salt into a bowl. Add 15 ml [1 tablespoon] melted butter and enough cold water to make a soft dough. Lightly knead the dough on a floured surface for a few minutes.

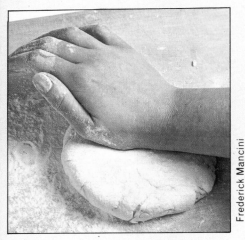

4 With floured hands, pat the dough out into a circle 18 cm [7"] in diameter.

5 Melt the remaining butter in a 20 cm [8"] frying-pan. Put the dough in the pan. Brown for 5 minutes on each side.

6 Heat the grill. Crumble the bacon and mix with the tomatoes and onions. Spoon over the top of the dough.

7 Arrange the sliced cheese on top of the tomatoes. Brown under a hot grill for 4 minutes. Garnish and serve cut into slices.

Cauliflower cheese soup

A new slant on an old favourite, this soup is hearty enough to serve alone for supper or lunch.

SERVES 4
⏳20 minutes
50 g [2 oz] Danish blue cheese
1 medium-sized cauliflower
225 g [½ lb] onions
850 ml [1½ pt] chicken stock
salt
freshly ground black pepper
4 thick slices of French bread

1 Grate the blue cheese. Wash and trim the leaves and trim away the stalk from the cauliflower. Divide into florets.

2 Peel and chop the onions. Put in a pan with the cauliflower and the stock plus the seasoning.

3 Simmer for 10 minutes. Purée in a blender.

4 Return to the pan. Add the cheese and heat gently, stirring until the cheese is melted.

5 Toast the bread and float on top of the soup.

German potato salad

Canned potatoes do not have much flavour unless treated in some way. Here is an ideal way to use them.

SERVES 4
⏳12 minutes
450 g [1 lb] pork sausages
225 g [½ lb] canned potatoes
2 large onions
1 large apple
salt
freshly ground black pepper
150 ml [¼ pt] soured cream

1 Fry the sausages. Heat the potatoes following the instructions on the can.

2 Meanwhile, peel and chop the onions and apple. Sauté for 2–3 minutes in the pan used for cooking the sausages.

3 Cut the potatoes into dice and the sausages into chunks.

4 Combine all ingredients and serve immediately.

This colourful Danish pizza makes an appetizing snack.

Alan Duns

Toast toppers

All of these will serve four.

● For Hawaiian rarebit, gradually melt 100 g [¼ lb] grated Cheddar cheese with 75 ml [3 fl oz] juice from 4-ring size canned pineapples and 5 ml [1 teaspoon] French mustard. Toast 4 slices of white bread. Place a pineapple ring on each. Pour the cheese mixture over and brown under a hot grill.

● For sausage and apple specials, grill or fry 8 large pork sausages. Toast 4 large slices of white bread. Spread with apple purée and top with the sausages sliced in half lengthways. Garnish with parsley.

● For creamed mushrooms on toast, thinly slice and sauté 100 g [¼ lb] button mushrooms. Stir 15 ml [1 tablespoon] plain flour into the pan with the mushrooms. Stir in 150 ml [¼ pt] thick cream and 5 ml [1 teaspoon] French mustard. Spoon mushroom mixture on to toast.

● For sunrise special, top slices of toast with sliced boiled ham and a fried egg. Garnish with parsley.

● For a Scandinavian treat, top toast with scrambled egg and thinly sliced Danish salami.

● For a beanfeast, top toast with baked beans mixed with crisply fried crumbled bacon and a little horseradish sauce.

● For Copenhagen toasts, top with 200 g [7 oz] canned sardines or pilchards. Peel, core and slice into rings 2 dessert apples and sauté the rings in butter. Pile on to the fish and top with a dollop of soured cream.

● For tuna and tomato toasts, top 4 toasts with 225 g [½ lb] sliced tomatoes brushed with butter. Grill until the tomatoes are soft. Spoon 90 g [3½ oz] drained tuna fish over the top. Garnish with celery leaves.

● For sweet Christmas toasts, top with 22 ml [1½ tablespoons] each of mincemeat and scatter over browned almonds.

● For Devon toasts, top with a good fruit jam and clotted cream.

A meal in a bun

Filling a hollowed roll with quickly cooked goodies provides an excellent lunch-box or evening snack.

SERVES 4
⧖ **20 minutes**
4 soft rolls
75 g [3 oz] butter
1 small onion
75 g [3 oz] button mushrooms
4 rashers streaky bacon
4 large eggs
60 ml [4 tablespoons] thick cream
salt
freshly ground black pepper

1 Heat the oven to 200°C [400°F] gas mark 6. Cut the tops off the rolls. Reserve. Scoop out the crumbs from the bottom half.

2 Use 50 g [2 oz] of the butter to coat the inside of the rolls.

3 Peel and chop the onion. Wipe and slice the mushrooms. Cut the bacon into strips. Fry bacon, onion and mushrooms in the remaining butter for 2–3 minutes.

4 Divide the mixture between the rolls. Break an egg into each roll. Spoon 15 ml [1 tablespoon] of cream over the top of each roll and season to taste. Replace top of each roll.

5 Place in an ovenproof dish and cook in the centre of the oven for 10 minutes.

Variations

● For springtime eggs, fill the base with chopped lettuce and sautéed onions.

● For Finnan eggs, fill the base with flaked, smoked haddock.

● For rosy eggs, fill the base with Italian tomato sauce.

Cheese fluffs

This elegant toast topper can be served as a first course at a dinner party if wished.

SERVES 4
⧖ **25 minutes**
4 slices of white bread
75 g [3 oz] strong Cheddar cheese
60 ml [4 tablespoons] thick cream
2.5 ml [½ teaspoon] French mustard
salt
freshly ground black pepper
1 large egg white

1 Toast the bread on both sides.

2 Meanwhile, grate the cheese and combine it with the cream, mustard, salt and black pepper.

3 Beat the egg white until it will stand in stiff peaks when the whisk is removed. Fold into the cheese mixture.

4 Pile the mixture on to the slices of toast. Brown under a hot grill for 3 minutes until golden and puffy.

Croque monsieur

The name of this dish means a 'man's munch' and it is more substantial than just a fried sandwich.

SERVES 4
⊠**12 minutes**
8 slices of white bread
75 g [3 oz] butter

4 thin slices lean ham
100 g [¼ lb] grated Cheddar cheese
oil for frying

1 Remove crusts from the bread. Spread four slices with butter.

2 Place a slice of ham on four of the slices of bread and cover with cheese. Top each with the remaining bread.

3 Heat the oil in a large frying-pan. Fry the sandwiches for 5 minutes on each side. Blot on kitchen paper before serving.

Irish scones

This scone batter is quick to make and does not need to stand. Be sure to cook the batter in the same fat as you used to fry the bacon in order to get a good flavour

SERVES 4
⊠**25 minutes**
For the batter:
60 ml [4 tablespoons] self-raising flour
salt
pepper
pinch of paprika
15 ml [1 tablespoon] freshly chopped chives
150 ml [¼ pt] milk
oil for frying

For the topping:
8 rashers streaky bacon
4 eggs

1 Sift the flour and seasonings into a bowl. Stir in the herbs.

2 Make a well in the centre. Beat in the milk to make a creamy batter.

3 Fry the bacon in the usual way. Reserve. Add oil to pan.

4 Drop the mixture 15 ml [1 tablespoon] at a time into the hot oil. When bubbles appear on the top, turn and cook the other side.

5 Keep scones hot while you fry the eggs. Arrange scones on a serving dish and layer bacon and eggs on top.

A selection of tasty toast toppers.

15

EGGS AND CHEESE

If you have a dozen eggs and some cheese in store, you may rest assured you will never be caught out when you are called on to make a hurried but delicious meal. Both ingredients can be used for plain family meals, such as fried or scrambled eggs or cheese on toast; but both are incredibly versatile. A soufflé omelette or a hot cheese salad look and taste as though you have been in the kitchen for hours, yet they hardly take any time at all to prepare.

Plain boiled eggs can be delicious at breakfast time, but for the main meal of the day, they might seem a little uninteresting. If you coat them with a thick and tasty sauce, such as an onion purée with cream, you can turn them into a meal that is delicious and attractive.

Two elaborate but quick ways with hard-boiled eggs—curried eggs with peanuts and eggs stuffed with ham.

Curried eggs with peanuts

Peanuts and sultanas are added to this curry sauce to make a really substantial meal for four. These ingredients marry extremely well with curry flavours. The rice completes the dish.

SERVES 4
⏳ 20 minutes
225 g [½ lb] long-grain rice
8 medium-sized eggs
50 g [2 oz] butter
100 g [¼ lb] unroasted peanuts
100 g [¼ lb] sultanas
15–30 ml [1–2 tablespoons] curry powder
30 ml [2 tablespoons] flour
575 ml [1 pt] milk

1 Place the rice in a saucepan with 575 ml [1 pt] water and 5 ml [1 teaspoon] salt.

2 Stir once then bring the water to the boil. Cover the pan and reduce heat so the water is simmering.

Leave to cook for about 15 minutes or until almost all the water has been absorbed and the rice is tender.

3 In the meantime, hard boil the eggs. Next, place the butter in a saucepan and heat gently until melted. Then stir in the peanuts, sultanas and curry powder to taste. Cook, stirring constantly, for 2 minutes.

4 Stir in the flour and cook for 2 minutes. Remove the pan from the heat and gradually stir in the milk.

5 Return to the heat and bring the sauce to the boil. Cook, stirring constantly, until the sauce is thick and smooth. Remove from the heat.

6 Drain the cooked rice then rinse in boiling water. Fluff the grains with a fork and turn into a shallow serving dish.

Frederick Mancini

7 To shell the eggs—gently tap all over to craze. Peel away central band, then slip off ends of shells. Cut eggs in half lengthways and arrange on top of the rice. Pour sauce over the eggs and serve.

Eggs stuffed with ham

Hard-boiled eggs are an excellent base for attractive cold dishes to serve with salad. Stuffed eggs look very professional, but take very little time to make if you prepare all the rest of the ingredients while the eggs are boiling. Home-made mayonnaise is best for this dish, but you can use a good quality, ready-prepared one.

SERVES 4
⧖ 35 minutes
8 medium-sized eggs
100 g [¼ lb] lean ham
4 medium-sized spring onions
175 ml [6 fl oz] thick mayonnaise
15 ml [1 tablespoon] Dijon mustard
crisp lettuce leaves
30 ml [2 tablespoons] freshly chopped parsley

1 Hard boil the eggs. Meanwhile, finely chop the ham and onions.

2 Drain the eggs and rinse in cold water. Shell, then cut in half lengthways.

3 Carefully scoop out the yolks then rub them through a nylon sieve.

4 Beat in 60 ml [4 tablespoons] of the mayonnaise and 10 ml [2 teaspoons] of the mustard. Stir in the chopped ham and onions.

5 Fill the eggs with the mayonnaise stuffing, then sandwich the halves together again.

6 Shred the lettuce leaves and lay over the base of a serving dish. Arrange the eggs on top of the lettuce.

7 Beat the parsley and remaining mustard into the rest of the mayonnaise and use to coat the eggs.

Poached eggs with orange and caper butter

Plainly poached eggs are lifted out of the ordinary when served on crispy fried bread and coated with a piquant sauce. As an alternative to the fried bread base suggested here, you could serve the eggs on cooked spinach, surrounded with tiny square croûtons.

SERVES 4
⧖ 25 minutes
8 medium-sized eggs
8 slices of white bread
100 g [¼ lb] butter
10 ml [2 teaspoons] wine vinegar or lemon juice
30 ml [2 tablespoons] chopped capers
grated zest and juice of 1 orange
45 ml [3 tablespoons] chopped parsley

1 Trim the crusts from the bread. Melt 50 g [2 oz] of the butter in a frying-pan. Fry the bread, a few slices at a time, until crisp and golden on both sides. Drain on kitchen paper and keep warm.

2 Pour water into a wide, shallow pan until it comes 5 cm [2"] up the side. Add the vinegar or lemon juice and bring to the boil, then reduce to simmering point. Swirl the water around.

Roger Phillips

3 Break the eggs, one at a time, into a saucer and slip into the water;

do not overcrowd the pan. Roll the egg over in the water with a perforated spoon to make sure the white encloses the yolk. Cook each one gently for 2 minutes until just set. Lift out with a perforated spoon, drain, then place on the fried bread.

4 Melt the remaining butter in the frying-pan over a high heat. When the foam subsides, add the capers, orange zest and juice and parsley. Cook for 15 seconds, then spoon over the eggs.

Salami scramble

Scrambled eggs are a good tasty standby in many households. Serve them plainly with slices of ham or soften other ingredients such as mushrooms in the butter before you stir in the eggs. Salami and green peppers give an Italian flavour. Either chips or sautéed potatoes will make excellent accompaniments.

SERVES 4
⧖ 25 minutes
8 medium-sized eggs
30 ml [2 tablespoons] tomato purée
salt
freshly ground black pepper
100 g [¼ lb] thinly sliced Italian salami
2 medium-sized green peppers
1 large onion
1 garlic clove
50 g [2 oz] butter

1 Crack the eggs into a bowl. Beat in the tomato purée and seasonings to taste.

2 Cut the slices of salami into quarters.

3 Core, de-seed and dice the peppers. Peel and thinly slice the onion and garlic.

4 Gently melt the butter in a heavy-based saucepan. Stir in the onion, garlic and peppers and cook gently until they become soft but are not coloured.

5 Add the salami to the pan. Stir in the eggs and cook gently, stirring constantly, until just set. Remove from the heat and serve the scramble mixture immediately.

Egg foo yung

Chinese beansprouts are increasingly popular. You can sprout them yourself or buy them fresh or canned. They can be made very quickly into egg dishes similar to those called foo yung in Chinese restaurants. Soy sauce is usually beaten into the eggs and a little curry powder is also added here for additional flavour. Serve with Special fried rice (page 30).

SERVES 4
⏳**15 minutes**
8 medium-sized eggs
30 ml [2 tablespoons] soy sauce
2 medium-sized onions
1 garlic clove
60 ml [4 tablespoons] groundnut oil
225 g [½ lb] beansprouts
10 ml [2 teaspoons] hot curry powder

1   Crack the eggs into a bowl, then beat in the soy sauce. Peel, then finely chop the onions and garlic.

2   Heat the oil in a large frying-pan over a high heat. Add the beansprouts, onions and garlic to the pan and fry quickly for 1 minute moving the vegetables continually with a pair of forks.

3   Sprinkle in the curry powder and mix in quickly. Pour in the eggs and cook, turning the mixture over with a spatula, until the eggs are just set.

Cauliflower and walnut cheese

This is cauliflower cheese with a difference. The cauliflower is braised with walnuts, then coated with a thick layer of grated cheese.

SERVES 4
⏳**25 minutes**
1 large cauliflower
1 large garlic clove
60 ml [4 tablespoons] olive oil
100 g [¼ lb] chopped walnuts
150 ml [¼ pt] stock
5 ml [1 teaspoon] dried thyme
225 g [½ lb] Double Gloucester cheese, grated

1   Remove leaves from the cauliflower, trim stalk and break cauliflower into small florets. Peel, then finely chop the garlic.

2   Pour the oil into a large frying-pan and set over a high heat. Add the garlic and walnuts and stir for 1 minute.

3   Add the cauliflower florets and turn in the oil. Pour in the stock and bring to the boil.

4   Add the thyme to the pan. Reduce the heat to moderate, cover the pan and cook for 10 minutes.

5   Turn the cauliflower and scatter the cheese over the top. Replace the lid, turn the heat to low and cook for 1 minute more. Serve immediately.

Frederick Mancini

Hot cheese and bacon ratatouille

This tasty, spicy dish makes an excellent accompaniment to cold cuts or grilled meat. Alternatively, serve as a light main course with a fresh green salad and crusty rolls.

SERVES 4
⏳**40 minutes**
225 g [½ lb] lean bacon
2 medium-sized onions
1 large garlic clove
30 ml [2 tablespoons] olive oil
350 g [¾ lb] courgettes
2 large red peppers
4 red chillies
225 g [½ lb] tomatoes
225 g [½ lb] Cheddar cheese, grated

1   Dice the bacon. Peel, then finely chop the onions and garlic.

2   Heat the oil gently in a large frying-pan. Add bacon, onions and garlic and cook for 5 minutes on a low heat.

3   Meanwhile, thinly slice the courgettes. Then core, de-seed and chop the peppers and chillies.

4   Add the courgettes, peppers and chillies to the pan, cover tightly and cook gently for 20 minutes.

5   Skin and roughly chop the tomatoes and add to the pan. Cover and cook for a further 5 minutes.

6   Heat the grill to moderate. Turn the contents of the pan into a gratin dish and scatter over the grated cheese. Place under the grill to melt the cheese then serve immediately.

Hot avocado and cheese salad

This is a bright and colourful salad with a superb blend of flavours. The cheese is added at the last minute—this way it heats through but remains firm.

SERVES 4
⏳**30 minutes**
2 firm avocados
225 g [½ lb] Cheshire cheese
450 g [1 lb] tomatoes
45 ml [3 tablespoons] white wine vinegar
10 ml [2 teaspoons] tomato purée
5 ml [1 teaspoon] paprika
dash Tabasco sauce
1 medium-sized lettuce
1 bunch watercress
8 medium-sized spring onions
1 large garlic clove
60 ml [4 tablespoons] olive oil
30 ml [2 tablespoons] freshly chopped parsley to garnish

1   Peel the avocados, cut in half lengthways and remove the stones. Cut each half thinly lengthways into strips.

2 Dice the cheese into 12 mm [½"] cubes. Slice the tomatoes into rounds. Beat the vinegar together with the tomato purée, paprika and Tabasco.

3 Tear the lettuce into small pieces; trim, then chop the watercress and spring onions. Arrange the lettuce, watercress and onions on one large serving dish or on four dinner plates.

4 Peel, then finely chop the garlic. Heat the oil and garlic in a large frying-pan over a high heat. When the garlic begins to sizzle, add the avocados and tomatoes and stir for 1 minute.

5 Add the cheese and stir for about 30 seconds so the cheese heats through but does not melt.

6 Pour in the vinegar mixture and allow it to bubble. Remove pan from the heat immediately and spoon the contents of the pan over the bed of lettuce, watercress and onions. Garnish with the freshly chopped parsley.

Baked cottage cheese savoury

A plain plate of cottage cheese for the slimmer is very easy to prepare but not very appetizing to eat! By adding a few extra ingredients you can create a hot, tasty dish that everyone will enjoy.

SERVES 4
⏲ **35 minutes**
450 g [1 lb] cottage cheese
2 medium-sized green peppers
30 ml [2 tablespoons] tomato purée
10 ml [2 teaspoons] paprika
15 ml [1 tablespoon] chopped fresh basil or parsley
450 g [1 lb] firm tomatoes
30 ml [2 tablespoons] browned breadcrumbs

1 Heat the oven to 200°C [400°F] gas mark 6.

2 Turn the cottage cheese into a bowl. Next core, de-seed and finely chop the peppers, then stir into the cottage cheese.

3 Add the tomato purée, paprika and herbs and stir until evenly blended.

4 Thinly slice the tomatoes.

5 Spread half the cheese mixture in the bottom of an ovenproof dish. Cover with half the sliced tomatoes. Spread the remaining cheese mixture evenly on top, then cover with the rest of the tomatoes.

6 Scatter the browned breadcrumbs over the surface and bake in the centre of the oven for 20 minutes.

Hot avocado and cheese salad makes a very elegant dinner-party dish.

Camembert toasts

Cheese on toast is one of those dishes that you always prepare when you cannot think of anything else—or when there is only bread and cheese in the cupboard. As a change from the more usual Cheddar, try some creamy Camembert, which will melt deliciously into the tomato purée.

SERVES 4
⌛20 minutes
8 slices of bread
50 g [2 oz] butter
approximately 30 ml [2 tablespoons] tomato purée
6 × 40 g [1½ oz] portions Camembert cheese

1 Trim the crusts from the bread, then toast the slices on one side.

2 Turn over and spread the untoasted side with butter and tomato purée.

Roger Phillips

3 Pare the rind from the cheese. Cut the cheese into slices and spread over the toast.

4 Toast under the grill until the cheese has melted.

Baked eggs with yoghurt

Baked eggs make a simple, yet tasty first course. They are a great standby for the busy cook, as they are easy to prepare and require the minimum of

Leek soufflé omelette makes a quick meal.

attention during cooking. Yoghurt provides a tangy contrast to the eggs. This recipe works particularly well with duck eggs. When available, fresh tarragon is a delicious alternative to parsley. Serve with fingers of buttered toast.

SERVES 4
⌛30 minutes
4 large eggs
15 g [½ oz] softened butter
75 ml [3 fl oz] plain yoghurt
salt
freshly ground black pepper
25 g [1 oz] grated Parmesan cheese
30 ml [2 tablespoons] freshly chopped parsley

1 Heat oven to 180°C [350°F] gas mark 4. Grease 4 ramekins with the butter.

2 Break an egg into each ramekin. Divide the yoghurt between the ramekins. Season with salt and pepper and sprinkle over the Parmesan and parsley.

3 Put the ramekins into a roasting pan. Pour in boiling water to half the depth of the ramekins. Cover the roasting pan with kitchen foil and bake for 15 minutes.

4 Remove foil and serve the eggs immediately.

Leek soufflé omelette

Soufflé omelettes look as though you have spent a considerable amount of time on them and yet they are almost as quick to prepare as ordinary omelettes. They are so light textured that they melt in the mouth. You can flavour them very simply with chopped herbs or add a small amount of filling. Instead of being filled and folded, this omelette includes leeks in the egg mixture and a topping of leeks and bacon.

The amounts given make an omelette for two—if you wish to serve four, double all the ingredients and use two pans simultaneously or keep the first omelette warm while you make the second. Soufflé omelettes can safely be kept warm for a short time as they do not sink like baked soufflés.

SERVES 2
⏳30 minutes
225 g [½ lb] leeks
2 streaky bacon rashers
25 g [1 oz] butter
4 large eggs
5 ml [1 teaspoon] Meaux mustard
salt
freshly ground black pepper

1 Wash the leeks well; drain, dry, then chop finely. Remove rind from bacon then cut into small pieces.

2 Melt half the butter in a pan over a low heat. Add leeks and bacon. Cook until leeks are soft.

Frederick Mancini

3 Remove from heat and leave to cool. Separate the eggs putting the whites into a separate clean, dry mixing bowl.

4 Beat the egg yolks and mustard together. Stir in half the cooled leek mixture. Add seasoning.

5 Beat the whites until they are stiff. Add the yolks to whites and fold in lightly.

6 Melt the remaining butter in a frying-pan over a medium heat. Heat the grill to moderate.

7 When foam subsides pour in the egg mixture. Cook for 60–90 seconds, without stirring, to set the bottom.

8 Place the pan under the grill to set and brown the top (about 2 minutes).

9 Spoon the remaining leeks over the top. Grill for another 30 seconds to heat through.

Mushroom omelette

Omelettes are quick to prepare and cook. This creamy textured mushroom and cheese omelette is easy to make for family meals yet delicious enough for guests as well. If you have any fresh chervil available it will impart a delicate nutty flavour.

SERVES 4
⏳30 minutes
350 g [¾ lb] button mushrooms
75 g [3 oz] butter
salt
freshly ground black pepper
8 medium-sized eggs
60 ml [4 tablespoons] freshly chopped parsley or chervil
100 g [¼ lb] Cheddar cheese, grated

1 Wipe, trim and thinly slice the mushrooms.

2 Melt 25 g [1 oz] of butter in a saucepan over a low heat. When the foam subsides, stir in the mushrooms and add seasoning. Cook gently for 3 minutes. Remove from heat and keep warm.

3 For each omelette, break 2 eggs into a bowl and add 15 ml [1 tablespoon] of parsley or chervil and seasoning. Beat lightly with a fork to mix the yolks with the whites.

4 Melt a quarter of the remaining butter in an omelette pan set over a high heat.

5 When the foam subsides, pour in the beaten eggs and stir the mixture with a fork, tilting the pan to ensure the whole base is covered evenly.

6 When the omelette is just set, spoon on a quarter of the mushrooms and a quarter of the cheese to one side.

7 Fold over the other side and slide the omelette on to a warm serving plate.

8 Keep it warm while you make the remaining omelettes in the same way.

Swiss soufflé

The flavour of this quick, classic dish can be varied by making different additions to the sauce.

SERVES 4
⏳ 50 minutes
275 ml [½ pt] milk
1.5 ml [¼ teaspoon] mustard powder
black pepper
pinch of grated nutmeg
pinch of cayenne pepper
25 g [1 oz] butter
25 g [1 oz] flour
4 medium-sized eggs
1 egg white
salt
75 g [3 oz] Cheddar, grated
75 g [3 oz] Gruyère, cubed

1 Heat the oven to 190°C [375°F] gas mark 5, and grease a 1.5 L [2¾ pt] soufflé dish.

2 Put the milk to warm in a small saucepan over a low heat and add the mustard, pepper, nutmeg and cayenne.

3 Melt the butter in a medium-sized saucepan over a low heat. Add the flour off the heat and stir to make a roux. Cook the roux for 1 minute.

4 Remove from the heat and add the warm milk, stirring until the sauce is smooth. Return to the heat and bring to the boil. Cook for 2 minutes, stirring, over low heat. Reserve.

5 Separate the eggs, putting the whites in a large dry bowl. Add the extra egg white. Beat with a pinch of salt until they will stand in stiff peaks.

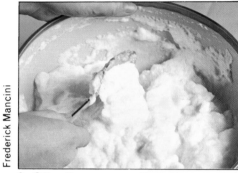

Frederick Mancini

6 Stir the egg yolks, the grated cheese and the cubed cheese into the sauce. Tip the sauce into the egg whites. Fold in with a metal spoon, using figure-of-eight movements, so that you cut through the mixture and gently enclose the sauce within the egg whites. Never beat, or you will lose all the air bubbles!

7 Turn the mixture immediately into the soufflé dish and bake in the centre of the oven for 35 minutes. Do not open the door until the end of the cooking time to have a look at it—otherwise the soufflé will collapse.

8 The soufflé is ready when it is risen and golden and just trembles in its dish if shaken gently. Serve immediately.

Variations

Change the flavour by omitting the cheese cubes in step 6 and adding any of the following to the sauce:
● 225 g [½ lb] mushrooms, sliced and gently sautéed in 25 g [1 oz] butter for 2–3 minutes. Drain off the mushroom juice before adding to the sauce with 15 ml [1 tablespoon] tomato ketchup.
● 175 g [6 oz] canned crab, drained of juice.
● 175 g [6 oz] poached, flaked, smoked haddock.
● 175 g [6 oz] cooked, diced ham or chicken.

Alan Duns

PERFECT PASTA

Easy and quick to cook, cheap and filling, pasta is a boon to the cook in a hurry. Pasta shapes can be used with a saucy dish to take the place of potatoes or other starchy vegetables and take only a fraction of the time to prepare. Pasta can also be used for 'one-pot dishes' such as cannelloni and lasagne (the Italian version of our own shepherd's pie).

Types of pasta
Pasta is available in a variety of shapes, from small patterns used in soups, to large sheets used for composite dishes. Regardless of shape, pasta can be divided into two categories. Pasta secco is made with durum wheat and water, while pasta all'uovo is made with durum wheat and egg. The latter has the better flavour, contains more protein and takes less time to cook than pasta secco. Some quick-cooking varieties are available. These have the advantage that dishes such as cannelloni and lasagne can be made without boiling the pasta first. Quick-cooking pasta is, therefore, a useful store-cupboard item—enabling you to put a hot meal together very quickly.

Quantities
Because pasta is filling, you do not need very much per person. If you are serving a dish such as noodles with bacon and cream as a first course, allow roughly 40 g [1½ oz] pasta per person. If you are serving it as a main course with, perhaps, a salad, increase the quantity by 15 g [½ oz]. If you want a filling meal based entirely on pasta, allow 100 g [¼ lb] per person. This is a generous quantity and you will satisfy the largest of appetites. Any left-over pasta can always be used cold in salads.

All the dishes given here will make an ample main course for four or a first course for six.

Cooking pasta
Pasta must be cooked in lots of boiling, salted water. In fact, the more water the better. The general rule is: 1.1 L [2 pt] water and 5 ml [1 teaspoon] salt for every 100 g [¼ lb] pasta. Keep the water boiling and do not cover the pan while the pasta is cooking.

To stop pasta sticking to itself, and also to give it a sheen, add a little oil or a knob of butter to the boiling water.

Pasta takes about 8–10 minutes to cook but always check the instructions on the packet—some types of pasta secco take much longer, while home-made pasta all'uovo can be cooked in as little as 5 minutes.

Do not overcook pasta—it is ready when a sample piece is 'al dente', that is, firm and still slightly resistant when you bite it. A minute too long and the pasta becomes soggy.

Mushroom macaroni cheese

A new slant on an old favourite, macaroni cheese with mushrooms makes a first-class high-protein meal. Serve with a crisp green or a mixed salad.

SERVES 4
⏳25–25 minutes
225 g [½ lb] macaroni
5 ml [1 teaspoon] oil
salt
40 g [1½ oz] butter
25 g [1 oz] plain flour
275 ml [½ pt] milk
150 ml [¼ pt] dry cider
5 ml [1 teaspoon] prepared mustard
100 g [¼ lb] mature Cheddar cheese
100 g [¼ lb] ham
75 g [3 oz] button mushrooms
freshly ground black pepper

1 Bring 2.3 L [4 pt] water to the boil. Add the oil and 10 ml [2 teaspoons] salt. Add the macaroni and cook for 8–10 minutes.

2 Meanwhile, melt 25 g [1 oz] of the butter in a heavy-based pan over a low heat. Stir in the flour and cook for 2 minutes.

3 Remove from heat and stir in the milk and cider. Then cook gently for 3 minutes, stirring until thickened. Stir in the mustard.

4 Grate the cheese and chop the ham. Add to the sauce. Remove sauce from the heat, cover and keep warm.

5 Melt the remaining butter in a small frying-pan. Wipe, slice and sauté the mushrooms. Mix into sauce. Check seasoning.

6 Heat the grill. Drain the macaroni and mix with the sauce in a heat-proof dish. Brown under the grill and serve immediately.

Store-cupboard lasagne

Made by the traditional method, lasagne takes quite a long time. Using canned mince and quick-cooking lasagne, the preparation and cooking time is reduced—and the results are delicious. Fresh mince can be used for the same recipe when you are less pressed for time. Fry it for 10 minutes in step 2.

SERVES 4
⏳40 minutes
225 g [½ lb] quick-cooking lasagne
15 ml [1 tablespoon] olive oil
1 large onion
2 garlic cloves
40 g [1½ oz] butter
225 g [½ lb] canned tomatoes
5 ml [1 teaspoon] dried oregano
225 g [½ lb] canned mince
salt
freshly ground black pepper
25 g [1 oz] flour
275 ml [½ pt] milk
75 g [3 oz] grated Parmesan cheese

1 Heat the oven to 190°C [375°] gas mark 5.

2 Heat olive oil in a heavy-based pan. Peel and chop the onion and the garlic and sauté in the olive oil.

3 Grease an ovenproof dish thickly

with 15 g [½ oz] of the butter. Arrange half the lasagne in the bottom of the dish.

4   Add the tomatoes, oregano, mince and salt and pepper to the onions. Cook for 5 minutes.

5   Meanwhile, melt the remaining butter in a pan and add the flour. Cook for one minute then stir in the milk. Bring to the boil, then lower the heat and cook for 2 minutes. Stir in 50 g [2 oz] of the cheese and check seasoning.

6   Spread half the mince over the lasagne and pour over half the sauce.

7   Cover with remaining lasagne. Add remaining mince and sauce. Sprinkle with remaining cheese and cook in the centre of the oven for 30 minutes.

Noodles with bacon and cream

This is quick and delicious dish. You can use another pasta instead of noodles or for a change use pasta verdi—that is pasta coloured green with spinach.

SERVES 4–6
⏳20–25 minutes
225 g [½ lb] noodles
salt
5 ml [1 teaspoon] oil
4 rashers streaky bacon
1 small onion
75 g [3 oz] mushrooms
1 large egg
150 ml [¼ pt] thick cream
50 g [2 oz] grated Parmesan cheese
freshly ground black pepper

1   Bring 2.3 L [4 pt] water to the boil. Add 10 ml [2 teaspoons] salt and the oil. Add the noodles and cook for 8–10 minutes.

2   Remove rind from bacon and cut rashers into small pieces. Fry in a heavy-based pan over a low heat until the fat runs.

3   Peel and chop the onion. Wipe and thinly slice the mushrooms. Sauté with the bacon for 4 minutes.

4   Drain the noodles. Beat the egg with cream and cheese. Season.

5   Stir the mixture into the noodles.

6   Stir in the cream and egg. Check seasoning and serve immediately.

Tagliatelle with meat balls

Meat balls are quick and easy to make but you can save time by using canned meat balls (add at step 7).

SERVES 4
⏳25 minutes
225 g [½ lb] tagliatelle
5 ml [1 teaspoon] oil
salt
50 g [2 oz] grated Parmesan cheese

For the meat balls:
350 g [¾ lb] minced beef
50 g [2 oz] mushrooms
half an onion
50 g [2 oz] breadcrumbs
1 large egg
30 ml [2 tablespoons] tomato purée
freshly ground black pepper
a little plain flour
25 g [1 oz] cooking fat

For the sauce:
225 g [½ lb] canned tomatoes
150 ml [¼ pt] chicken stock
2 garlic cloves
5 ml [1 teaspoon] dried oregano

1   To make the meat balls, fork through the mince to break it up.

2 Wipe and trim the mushrooms. Peel the onion. Finely chop or mince the onion and mushrooms and add to the minced beef.

3 Add the breadcrumbs. Beat the egg with the tomato purée and stir in. Season with salt and pepper.

4 With floured hands form the mince into balls about the size of golf balls.

A selection of pastas. From left to right— Top row: pasta wheels, lasagne, tagliatelle verdi and lasagne verdi. Bottom row: pasta spirals, pasta shells, cannelloni tubes, elbow macaroni, Chinese egg noodles and long spaghetti.

5 Melt the cooking fat in a large frying-pan over a low heat. Increase heat, add the meat balls to the pan and cook, turning to seal all sides, for 5 minutes. Lift out with a slotted spoon, drain on kitchen paper and keep warm.

6 To make the sauce, add the tomatoes and stock to the pan. Peel, then crush the garlic cloves with a little salt and add to the pan. Stir in the oregano and check seasoning. Bring to the boil then reduce heat.

7 Return the meat balls to the pan and simmer in the sauce for 10 minutes.

8 Meanwhile, bring 2.3 L [4 pt] water to the boil. Add the oil and 10 ml [2 teaspoons] salt. Add the tagliatelli and cook for 8–10 minutes.

9 Drain the tagliatelle. Arrange around the edge of a warmed serving dish. Put the meat balls and sauce in the centre. Sprinkle with Parmesan cheese.

Chicken tetrazzini

This Italian dish is quick to make because it uses left-over chicken. Turkey or ham may be used instead.

Tagliatelle with meat balls is a traditional Italian-American dish. Use any variety of pasta you wish.

SERVES 4
⏳ 25 minutes
225 g [½ lb] spaghetti
5 ml [1 teaspoon] oil
salt
100 g [¼ lb] button mushrooms
25 g [1 oz] butter
225 g [½ lb] canned
   tomatoes
1 garlic clove
freshly ground black pepper

For the sauce:
350 g [¾ lb] cooked chicken
   meat
25 g [1 oz] butter
25 g [1 oz] plain flour
150 ml [¼ pt] chicken stock
150 ml [¼ pt] milk
75 ml [3 fl oz] white wine
50 g [2 oz] grated Parmesan
   cheese

1 Bring 2.3 L [4 pt] water to the boil.

2 In the meantime, prepare the chicken sauce. Cut the chicken meat into chunks and set aside.

3 Melt the butter in a heavy-based pan over a low heat. Stir in the flour.

4 Gradually incorporate the stock, milk and wine. Bring to the boil and cook for a few minutes until thickened and smooth, stirring constantly.

5 Stir in the chicken and cheese and season to taste. Set the mixture aside.

6 Add the oil and 10 ml [2 teaspoons] salt to the boiling water. Add the spaghetti and cook for 8 minutes.

7 Meanwhile, wipe and slice the mushrooms. Melt 25 g [1 oz] butter in a heavy-based pan. Sauté the mushrooms for 2 minutes taking care they do not overcook.

8 Add the canned tomatoes. Peel and crush the garlic clove and add. Season to taste. Simmer, uncovered, for 5 minutes. Meanwhile put the chicken mixture on to reheat.

9· Drain the spaghetti. Toss in the tomato sauce. Arrange around the edge of a heated serving dish. Pour the chicken sauce into the centre of the dish and serve immediately.

Pasta shells with tuna

Italians are very fond of tuna and it goes well with pasta. This is a dish that is quickly made. Serve with a crisp, green salad—it is an accompaniment that offers an excellent contrast in texture.

SERVES 4
⏳15 minutes
**225 g [½ lb] pasta shells
salt
5 ml [1 teaspoon] oil
225 g [½ lb] canned tuna fish
3 large ripe tomatoes
1 garlic clove
15 ml [1 tablespoon] olive oil
freshly ground black pepper**

1 Bring 2.3 L [4 pt] water to the boil. Add 10 ml [2 teaspoons] salt and the oil. Add pasta shells and cook for 8–10 minutes.

2 Drain and flake the tuna. Skin, deseed and chop the tomatoes. Peel and crush the garlic clove with a little salt.

Frederick Mancini

3 Heat the olive oil in a small frying-pan. Sauté the tomatoes and garlic for 3 minutes. Add the tuna. Heat through and correct seasoning.

4 Drain the pasta and toss with the tuna mixture. Serve immediately.

Pasta wheels and sausage feast

Instead of sausages and mash, try sausages and pasta. Time is saved because there is none of the preparation associated with mashed potatoes.

SERVES 4
⏳20 minutes
**225 g [½ lb] pasta wheels
salt
5 ml [1 teaspoon] oil
15 g [½ oz] cooking fat
450 g [1 lb] sausages
1 large onion
1 small green pepper
275 ml [½ pt] canned tomato
   soup
pinch of oregano
freshly ground black pepper**

1 Bring 2.3 L [4 pt] water to the boil. Add 10 ml [2 teaspoons] salt and the oil. Add pasta and cook for 8–10 minutes.

2 Meanwhile, melt the fat in a heavy-based frying-pan. Prick the sausages with a fork, then fry until lightly browned—about 5 minutes.

3 Peel and chop the onion. De-seed the green pepper then dice.

4 Lift the sausages from the pan, drain on absorbent kitchen paper then cut in slices 5 cm [2"] thick.

5 Add the onion and green pepper to the pan and cook gently until soft but not brown. Add the tomato

soup and oregano, together with the sausage pieces. Season to taste. Simmer for 5 minutes.

6 Drain the pasta and arrange around edge of a heated dish. Pour sausage mixture into centre.

Pasta and pineapple salad

Left-over pasta need not go to waste—it can be used to make a quick and delicious salad.

SERVES 4
⏳5 minutes
**175 g [6 oz] cold cooked pasta
   shells
175 g [6 oz] canned pineapple
   pieces
30 ml [2 tablespoons] olive oil
5 ml [1 teaspoon] Dijon or
   Meaux mustard
salt
freshly ground black pepper
1 small green pepper
100 g [¼ lb] cooked ham,
   chicken or turkey meat**

1 Put the pasta shells in a bowl. Drain the pineapple pieces, reserving the juice. Add the pineapple chunks to the pasta shells.

2 To make the vinaigrette, mix 45 ml [3 tablespoons] of the reserved pineapple juice with the oil. Whisk in the mustard. Season to taste.

3 De-seed the green pepper and chop finely. Cut the meat into chunks. Mix with the pasta.

4 Add the vinaigrette and toss the salad before serving.

Pasta twists in cream cheese

This is a very rich, but light, appetizer. Serve with a bowl of Parmesan.

SERVES 4
⏳15–20 minutes
**175 g [6 oz] pasta twists
salt
5 ml [1 teaspoon] oil
30 ml [2 tablespoons] freshly
   snipped chives
100 g [¼ lb] full fat cream
   cheese
freshly ground black pepper
50 g [2 oz] walnuts
50 g [2 oz] butter**

1 Bring 1.7 L [3 pt] water to the boil. Add 5 ml [1 teaspoon] salt and the oil and cook the pasta for 8–10 minutes.

2 In the meantime, beat the chives into the cream cheese. Season with salt and plenty of freshly ground black pepper.

3 Chop the walnuts. Drain the cooked pasta and toss immediately in the butter and then add the cream cheese. Mix in the walnuts and serve at once.

Variation
● For pasta in creamy mushroom sauce, omit the chives, cream cheese and walnuts. Fry 2 rashers chopped back bacon with 50 g [2 oz] sliced mushrooms. Add 100 g [¼ lb] cooked peas and 75 ml [3 fl oz] thin cream and heat through gently. Add the cooked, drained pasta and toss well.

Pasta shells and tuna combine deliciously.

WAYS WITH RICE

Like pasta, rice is easy to cook and versatile. It can be mixed with other ingredients to make tasty, inexpensive, one-pot meals; served as an accompaniment to soups, curries and similar dishes or used to stretch small amounts of meat (see pork and rice casserole, page 31).

Rice is very quick to cook and makes a filling dish. It is also very easy to prepare because no peeling or slicing is necessary.

Most of the rice bought today is white long-grain, easy-cook rice. This type of rice is specially treated so that it cooks quickly and the grains remain separate. Rice expands on cooking—so much so, that if you start off with 100 g [¼ lb] you will end up with about 350 g [¾ lb] at the end of cooking. As a guide when serving rice, allow 25–50 g [1–2 oz] (raw weight) per person, depending on the quantity of other ingredients being used.

To cook rice, follow the manufacturer's instructions carefully. Always cook covered and never stir more than once. It is stirring that makes rice sticky. The amount of water used should be in proportion to the rice—usually 275 ml [½ pt] to cook 100 g [¼ lb] rice. Do not use more water or the cooked rice will be soggy. The water should be salted, 2.5–5 ml [½–1 teaspoon] salt is generally sufficient.

For the recipes in this chapter, always use white long-grain, easy-cook rice. Brown rice, delicious as it is, is not suitable when preparing quick meals, because it takes too long to cook.

Frederick Mancini

This paella made from store-cupboard ingredients tastes and looks like the real thing.

Kedgeree

This was originally a breakfast dish but nowadays it is more usually served as a main course with a salad.

SERVES 4
⏳30 minutes
4 rashers streaky bacon
75 g [3 oz] button mushrooms
4 large eggs
100 g [¼ lb] long-grain rice
salt
a large pinch of turmeric
225 g [½ lb] boil-in-the-bag smoked haddock
15 g [½ oz] butter
freshly ground black pepper

To garnish:
sliced tomato
freshly chopped parsley

1 Remove the rind from the bacon and cut the rashers into strips. Sauté until the fat runs freely. Wipe and slice the mushrooms. Sauté with the bacon for 1 minute. Set aside.

2 Hard boil the eggs. Cook the rice in twice its volume of boiling salted water for 12 minutes, adding a pinch of turmeric to give colour.

3 Cook the fish following the manufacturer's instructions. Turn into a bowl with any juices and flake with a fork.

4 Drain the rice if necessary. Add the rice and the fish to the mushroom and bacon mixture. Set over low heat.

5 Shell and quarter the eggs and add to the rice mixture. Stir in the butter and check the seasoning. Heat through gently.

6 Arrange the tomato slices around the edge of a warm serving plate. Turn the kedgeree into the centre and garnish with freshly chopped parsley.

Quick paella

Traditional Spanish paella takes a long time to make. This version can be made in minutes using store cupboard ingredients. It is an economical paella and does not include the customary saffron and chicken, nor the garnish of fresh shellfish but the result is just as pretty and colourful. It looks and tastes as good cold.

SERVES 4
⏳35–40 minutes
2 large onions
50 g [2 oz] butter
225 g [½ lb] long-grain rice
575 ml [1 pt] chicken stock
pinch of turmeric
1 green pepper
75 g [3 oz] canned pimento
225 g [½ lb] canned tuna
225 g [½ lb] canned or frozen prawns
100 g [¼ lb] frozen peas
salt
freshly ground black pepper

To garnish:
lemon wedges
2 tomatoes, sliced
freshly chopped parsley

1 Peel and chop the onions. Melt the butter in a heavy-based pan over a low heat. Sauté the onion for 2 minutes.

2 Stir in the rice. Stir for 2 minutes until well coated with butter.

3 Add the stock and the turmeric. Bring to the boil then reduce heat. Core, de-seed and chop the green pepper. Drain the pimento then cut into strips. Add to the pan with the green pepper.

4 Cover and simmer for 10 minutes. Drain the tuna and prawns. Add to the pan with the peas. Simmer for a further 10 minutes until all the liquid had evaporated.

5 Check seasoning. Serve from the pan, garnished with lemon wedges, sliced tomato and the chopped parsley.

Frederick Mancini

Ham and rice roulade

This is a quick supper dish for two. If you have no cooked long-grain rice available, use minute rice. This can be reconstituted and ready to eat in under 5 minutes.

SERVES 2
⏳20 minutes
2 slices cooked ham
2 thin slices Gruyère cheese
50 g [2 oz] cooked long-grain rice
25 g [1 oz] butter
25 g [1 oz] flour
275 ml [½ pt] milk
50 g [2 oz] Parmesan cheese
salt
freshly ground black pepper

1 Lay the ham on a flat surface. Cover each slice with a slice of Gruyère cheese.

2 Divide the rice between the slices. Roll up and secure with a cocktail stick.

3 Melt the butter in a heavy-based pan over a low heat. Stir in the flour and cook for 2 minutes.

4 Gradually incorporate the milk. Bring to the boil and cook gently, stirring continuously, for 5 minutes. Stir in the Parmesan cheese. Season to taste.

5 Heat the grill. Arrange the ham rolls in a greased flameproof dish. Pour over the sauce. Brown under the grill.

Turkey à la king

This is a good dish to serve during the festive season when plain cold turkey begins to pall.

SERVES 4
⌛30 minutes
450 g [1 lb] cooked turkey
   meat
75 g [3 oz] mushrooms
1 onion
1 red pepper
50 g [2 oz] butter
100 g [¼ lb] long-grain rice
salt
75 g [3 oz] frozen peas
25 g [1 oz] plain flour
275 ml [½ pt] milk
150 ml [¼ pt] white wine
150 ml [¼ pt] thick cream
freshly ground black pepper
50 g [2 oz] salted peanuts,
   chopped

1 Dice the turkey meat. Wipe, trim, then slice the mushrooms. Peel and chop the onion. Core, deseed, then chop the red pepper.

2 Melt half the butter in a heavy-based pan. Add the mushrooms, onion and pepper and cook until soft. Set aside.

3 Cook the rice in twice its volume of boiling, salted water for 12 minutes. Add the peas to the rice 2–3 minutes before the end of cooking.

4 Meanwhile, melt the remaining butter in a small heavy-based pan over a low heat. Remove from heat and stir in the flour. Then cook for 2 minutes.

5 Gradually incorporate the milk, wine and cream. Season with salt and pepper. Bring to the boil, reduce heat and cook gently, stirring constantly, for 5 minutes. Stir the turkey into the sauce together with the softened vegetables. Check seasoning.

6 Drain the rice if necessary. Arrange around the edge of a warm serving dish. Pour the sauce into the centre and sprinkle over the nuts. Serve.

A selection of filling, quick-cooking rice dishes—chicken and peach salad, pork and rice casserole and special fried rice.

Special fried rice

This is a variation of the rice dish most people associate with Chinese food. The rice must be part-boiled first, otherwise it will not cook through. Diced ham may be used in place of the chicken if preferred.

SERVES 4
⌛20 minutes
100 g [¼ lb] long-grain rice
salt
50 g [2 oz] butter
75 g [3 oz] button mushrooms
75 g [3 oz] cooked chicken
   meat
75 g [3 oz] shelled prawns
2 large eggs

1 Cook the rice in twice its volume of boiling, salted water for 8 minutes.

2 In the meantime, melt the butter in a heavy-based frying-pan. Wipe and slice the mushrooms. Sauté in the butter for 2 minutes.

3 Dice the chicken meat. Add to the pan, together with the prawns. Stir the ingredients to mix.

4 Drain the rice and add to the pan. Cook for 3 minutes, stirring constantly.

5 Beat the eggs. Pour into the pan in a thin stream, stirring all the time, so that the egg sets in little pieces. Serve at once.

Chicken and peach salad

This is a good way to use leftovers, but the salad is so delicious you may want to prepare the ingredients specially for it. If there is no cooked rice available, use minute rice instead. Run cold water through it to cool and then spread it out on a plate after draining. Cooked ham or turkey may be used instead of the chicken if wished.

SERVES 4
⌛10 minutes
450 g [1 lb] cooked chicken
   meat
225 g [½ lb] cooked long-grain
   rice
45 ml [3 tablespoons] French
   dressing
400 g [14 oz] canned peach
   halves
25 g [1 oz] leek, chopped
salt
freshly ground black pepper
40 g [1½ oz] Philadelphia
   cheese
25 g [1 oz] chopped walnuts

1 Cut the chicken meat into bite-sized pieces and mix with the cold rice. Toss in the French dressing.

Frederick Mancini

Frederick Mancini

2 Drain the peach halves. Set four aside. Chop the remainder and mix with the rice, chicken and leek. Check seasoning.

3 Fill cavities of the reserved peach halves with cream cheese. Cut each in half. Arrange on top of the rice salad.

4 Sprinkle with chopped walnuts.

Pork and rice casserole

One of the great advantages of rice is that it can be used to stretch more expensive food such as meat. Here is a way to make two pork chops serve four people. The rendered fat is left in the dish to add succulence and flavour.

SERVES 4
⏳ 50 minutes
2 large pork chops
1 onion
1 garlic clove
1 green pepper
75 g [3 oz] button mushrooms
275 ml [½ pt] canned tomato
   soup
100 g [¼ lb] long-grain rice
pinch of oregano
salt
freshly ground black pepper

1 Heat the oven to 190°C [375°F] gas mark 5.

2 Peel and chop the onion and garlic. Core, de-seed, then chop the green pepper. Wipe, trim, then slice the mushrooms.

3 Set a heavy-based flameproof casserole over moderate heat. Trim excess fat from the chops. Place the fat trimmings in the casserole and fry until the fat runs freely.

Alan Duns

4 Dice the chops, and add to the pan. Increase heat and brown the meat on all sides. Reduce heat.

5 Add the onion to the pan and cook until soft but not brown. Add the garlic, green pepper and mushrooms and cook for 3 minutes. Stir in the tomato soup.

6 Stir in the rice and oregano, then season to taste.

7 Cover and cook in the oven for 40 minutes or until the rice is just tender and the liquid is absorbed.

MEAT IN MINUTES

It is not only the more expensive cuts that can be cooked quickly. Offal and chicken, both of which are always cheap, can also be cooked in under 30 minutes (see recipes). If you have no fresh meat in the house and have to provide a meal, try these ideas using canned meat.

Fritters
● Spam, luncheon meat and corned beef can all be coated in fritter or ordinary batter and deep-fried. Serve with a home-made tomato sauce.

Saucy dishes
● Canned ham, chicken or tongue can be cubed and mixed with lightly sautéed onion, sliced sautéed mushrooms and a good cheese, parsley or other white sauce, then served with rice or used as a filling. Frozen vol-au-vents are quick to bake.
● All of these meats can also be cut into chunks and set in layers in aspic jelly. Packeted aspic is quick to prepare and if you set the mould in the freezer compartment of your refrigerator, it will be firm in 30 minutes.
● These meats may also be minced and used as the base for a soufflé, or rolled up in pancakes.

Canned mince
Canned mince is not very exciting, but with a little imagination it can be transformed into tasty dishes.
● For instant chilli con carne, peel, chop and sauté an onion and garlic clove in butter. Add 425 g [15 oz] canned mince, 425 g [15 oz] canned kidney beans and a dash of Tabasco sauce. Simmer for 15–20 minutes and serve on a bed of boiled rice.
● To make a mild curry, stir 30 ml [2 tablespoons] curry paste into 425 g [15 oz] canned mince. Add 50 g [2 oz] raisins and 15 ml [1 tablespoon] desiccated coconut.
● For korma curry, stir 150 ml [¼ pt] natural yoghurt into the mild curry given above.

Corned beef hash

Canned corned beef is very uninteresting served alone but with the addition of other ingredients, it can be made into a delicious meal for four.

This recipe uses canned potatoes
for a real emergency; when you are less pressed, use fresh potatoes—allow an extra 20 minutes of preparation time. Peel about 700 g [1½ lb] and cut into 2.5 ml [1″] cubes. Boil in salted water until tender. Drain well.*

SERVES 4
⧖ 30 minutes
450 g [1 lb] canned potatoes
30 ml [2 tablespoons] oil
1 large onion
425 g [15 oz] canned baked beans in tomato sauce
350 g [¾ lb] canned corned beef
parsley to garnish

1 Slice the potatoes. Fry in the oil until golden. Drain and set aside.

2 Peel and chop the onion and fry in the same oil. Set aside.

3 Mix the potato and onion together. Pour the beans into a bowl. Cube the corned beef and mix with the beans. Mix in all but a quarter of the potato and onion mixture.

4 Simmer on top of the stove until heated through—about 10 minutes. Heat the grill.

5 Sprinkle the mixture with the reserved potato and onion and brown under a hot grill for 5 minutes. Sprinkle with parsley.

Children will love this tasty corned beef hash which takes the minimum amount of time to prepare and cook.

Frankfurter beanfeast

A guaranteed favourite with children, this involves little preparation.

SERVES 4
⧖ 20 minutes
425 g [15 oz] canned baked beans in tomato sauce
150 ml [¼ pt] stock
30 ml [2 tablespoons] tomato purée
5 ml [1 teaspoon] soft brown sugar
pinch of mustard
salt
freshly ground black pepper
1 medium-sized onion
15 g [½ oz] butter
225 g [½ lb] frankfurters

1 Blend the stock with the tomato purée, sugar and mustard. Season lightly with salt and pepper.

2 Peel, then finely chop the onion. Melt the butter in a heavy-based saucepan, add the onions and cook gently until soft but not brown.

3 Add the beans to the pan together with the flavoured stock. Slice the frankfurters and add to sauce.

4 Stir the ingredients together. Cover the pan and cook gently for about 5 minutes to heat through.

5 Check the seasoning and transfer to a warmed serving dish.

David Levin

Savoury mince mixture

This basic savoury mince can be used as a base for bolognese sauce, a filling for lasagne, the base of a shepherd's pie or for a moussaka.

Use canned mince in emergencies. Add it in step 3 with the other ingredients and you will cut 10 minutes off preparation time.

SERVES 4
⏳ 30 minutes
225 g [½ lb] mince
1 small onion
1 garlic clove
100 g [¼ lb] fresh or tinned
    mushrooms
25 g [1 oz] butter
100 g [¼ lb] canned tomatoes
30 ml [2 tablespoons] tomato
    purée
salt
freshly ground black pepper
5 ml [1 teaspoon] dried
    oregano or basil

1 Peel and chop the onion. Peel and crush the garlic. Wipe and slice the mushrooms if fresh.

2 Melt the butter in a heavy-based pan. Sauté the onion, garlic and mushrooms for 4 minutes over low heat. Stir in the mince and fry for 10 minutes.

3 Add all the other ingredients and simmer for 10 minutes, stirring from time to time.

Using the mince mixture
● For moussaka, layer in a dish with 450 g [1 lb] sliced canned potatoes. Make up a white sauce using 275 ml [½ pt] milk, 25 g [1 oz] butter and 25 g [1 oz] flour. Add 50 g [2 oz] grated cheese. Beat into it 1 egg and use to top the dish. Cook in the oven for 30 minutes at 220°C [425°F] gas mark 7.
● For spaghetti bolognese, serve with 225 g [½ lb] boiled, buttered spaghetti.

● For shepherd's pie topping, put 700 g [1½ lb] potatoes to boil. Start the mince and while it is cooking, chop 1 small onion finely and soften it in 25 g [1 oz] butter in another pan for 4 minutes. Add 50 ml [2 fl oz] milk and bring to the boil. Then add the drained potatoes and either mash or purée in a blender. Season and use to top the mince in a dish. Brown under the grill or in oven.

Stir-fried beef

The secret of successful Chinese cooking is to prepare everything in front. The actual cooking is very quick indeed. Serve with crispy Chinese noodles or plain boiled rice.

SERVES 4
⏳25 minutes
450 g [1 lb] fillet or top rump beef
30 ml [2 tablespoons] seasoned flour
275 ml [½ pt] stock, from beef cube
1 cauliflower, or 1 parsnip
1 large onion
2 celery stalks
50 g [2 oz] butter
30 ml [2 tablespoons] oil
30 ml [2 tablespoons] soy sauce
salt
freshly ground black pepper

1 Cut the meat into thin strips. Toss in the seasoned flour.

2 Heat the stock in a large pan. Wash and cut the cauliflower into florets or cut the parsnip into 2.5 cm [1"] cubes. Add the cauliflower florets or parsnips to the pan and bring to the boil. Cook for 3 minutes.

3 Peel and slice the onion. Wash and chop the celery. Heat the butter and oil in a frying-pan and fry the onion and celery over medium heat for 2 minutes.

4 Add the meat strips and fry with the onion and celery, stirring every now and then, until brown. Add the soy sauce and continue frying over a high heat for 1 minute, stirring all the time.

5 Add the cauliflower or parsnips to the frying-pan and then the stock. Reduce the heat and simmer for 2 minutes stirring occasionally. Season and serve.

Beef stroganoff

This is the classic fast dinner-party dish—but you must use the very best steak for it to be really tender and tasty. If soured cream is not available stir 5 ml [1 teaspoon] of lemon juice into double cream.

SERVES 4
⏳10 minutes
450 g [1 lb] fillet steak
100 g [¼ lb] button mushrooms
50 g [2 oz] butter
150 ml [¼ pt] soured cream
freshly chopped parsley to garnish

1 Cut the steak into thin strips.

2 Wipe and thinly slice the mushrooms. Melt the butter in a large, heavy-based frying-pan over a medium heat.

3 Add the steak and mushrooms and sauté for 5 minutes. Stir in the soured cream. Serve at once garnished with freshly chopped parsley.

Shish kebabs

This delicious Middle-Eastern speciality is increasingly popular. To serve, arrange the skewers on a bed of freshly boiled rice or noodles and pour over the basting juices.

SERVES 4
⏳35 minutes
700 g [1½ lb] boned, cubed shoulder of lamb
50 ml [2 fl oz] olive oil
30 ml [2 tablespoons] lemon juice
1 garlic clove
salt
2.5 ml [½ teaspoon] cinnamon
2.5 ml [½ teaspoon] black pepper
pinch of paprika
pinch of cayenne
2 medium-sized onions
4 tomatoes
8 bay leaves

1 Choose a large gratin dish suitable for serving. Pour the olive oil and lemon juice into the dish.

2 Peel and chop the garlic, then crush with a little salt until it forms a smooth paste. Stir into the olive oil and lemon juice together with the cinnamon, black pepper, paprika and cayenne.

3 Trim any large chunks of fat from the lamb and discard. Cut the meat roughly into 4 cm [1½"] cubes if necessary. Turn the meat in the sauce until evenly coated.

4 Peel, then thickly slice the onions into rings. Keep the slices intact—do not push out into rings. Cut the tomatoes in half across the middle. Turn the onion and tomato in the oil mixture until well coated. Add the bay leaves and turn in the oil mixture.

5 Oil four long skewers. Thread the ingredients on to the skewers, in the following way: a meat cube, bay leaf, meat cube, tomato, meat cube, onion. Continue in this way until all the meat is used up. Do not pack too closely or cooking time will be lengthened.

6 Heat the grill to medium. Arrange the skewers so they balance across the gratin dish (to catch the drips). Baste with any remaining sauce.

7 Place under the grill 7.5 cm [3"] beneath the heat and grill for 10 minutes on each side. Turn with tongs and baste frequently.

Pork chops with prunes

Buy ready-plumped or the non-soak variety of Californian prunes for this recipe, to cut the soaking time. You will need the lesser weight if they are already stoned.

SERVES 4
⏳40 minutes
4 pork chops
100–175 g [4–6 oz] prunes
1 medium-sized onion
15 ml [1 tablespoon] flour
15 ml [1 tablespoon] white wine vinegar
15 ml [1 tablespoon] jelly marmalade
pinch of nutmeg
salt
freshly ground black pepper

1 Put the prunes in a pan and pour over boiling water to just cover. Simmer gently until required.

2 Peel, then finely chop the onion. Trim the fat from the pork chops, chop it finely and put in a large, heavy-based frying-pan. Fry the fat over medium heat until the fat runs out and the bits become crisp. Remove bits and discard.

3 Add the pork chops and fry for 3 minutes on each side until coloured.

4 Add the onion and reduce the heat to low. Cook a further 3 minutes. Drain the prunes, reserving 150 ml [¼ pt] of the liquid.

5 Sprinkle flour into pan and add the reserved liquid, the vinegar, jelly marmalade, nutmeg, salt and the drained prunes.

6 Cover and simmer for 20–30 minutes. Check seasoning and serve.

Spare ribs

Buy lean spare rib chops for this dish, not the Chinese-style spare ribs which are bones with very little meat attached. Spare rib chops are lean but less tender than loin or chump chops. If you have time make Croûtons—crispy cubes of freshly fried bread—as they make a good contrast to the rich meat. Serve them sprinkled over the meat.

SERVES 4
⏳ 45 minutes
700 g [1½ lb] spare rib chops
2 medium-sized onions
15 g [½ oz] butter
225 g [½ lb] dessert apples
2 cloves
large pinch ground ginger
large pinch grated nutmeg
2.5 ml [½ teaspoon] paprika
45 ml [3 tablespoons]
    concentrated orange juice
15 ml [1 tablespoon] Demerara
    sugar
salt
freshly ground black pepper

1 Remove the bone, then chop the meat into 2.5 cm [1"] cubes. Peel, then finely chop the onions.

2 Melt the butter in a large frying-pan over low heat and add the meat. Cook, turning, for 10 minutes to let the fat run out.

3 Move the meat to one side, add the onions and turn them in the fat. Continue frying both meat and onions for a further 10 minutes.

4 Meanwhile, peel, core and chop the apples. Add to the pan, together with the spices.

5 Mix the orange juice with 200 ml [7 fl oz] water. Stir in the sugar, then pour into the pan. Season to taste with salt and pepper and simmer for about 20 minutes. Serve immediately.

Stir-fried beef—a Chinese meal to impress your family and friends.

Cumberland lamb chops

The sweet taste of oranges goes well with lamb, while stewing gently in the pan will help to tenderize chops. Use loin or chump chops.

SERVES 4
⧗ **40 minutes**
4 lamb chops
15–30 ml [1–2 tablespoons] oil
1 medium-sized onion
2 oranges
5 ml [1 teaspoon] cornflour
15 ml [1 tablespoon] Dijon mustard
60 ml [4 tablespoons] redcurrant jelly
50 ml [2 fl oz] medium sherry, red vermouth or port
salt
freshly ground black pepper

1 Pour the oil into a large frying-pan over a medium heat. Add the chops and fry for 3 minutes on each side until coloured.

2 Peel, then chop the onion. Add to the pan, reduce the heat to low and cook for 4 minutes until the onions are soft but not brown.

3 Meanwhile, thickly grate zest of one orange and squeeze the juice of both. Put the cornflour into a small bowl. Add the orange juice and mustard and blend to a smooth paste. Add to the pan together with the zest and jelly.

4 Bring to the boil, stirring to break up the jelly. Add the medium sherry, red vermouth or port and 50 ml [2 fl oz] water. Reduce the heat to low, cover and simmer for 20 minutes.

5 Check the seasoning. Lift the chops on to a warm serving plate. If necessary, boil the sauce to reduce it further then spoon over.

Turkey escalopes

Turkey breast meat is increasingly available in supermarkets and it is cheaper than the classic veal escalopes.

SERVES 4
⧗ **25 minutes**
450 g [1 lb] turkey breast meat
30 ml [2 tablespoons] lemon juice
salt
freshly ground black pepper
50 g [2 oz] seasoned flour
50 g [2 oz] butter
20 ml [4 teaspoons] oil
60 ml [4 tablespoons] sweet sherry or Marsala
45 ml [3 tablespoons] grated Parmesan cheese
60 ml [4 tablespoons] chicken stock

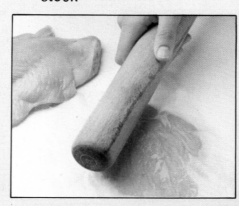

1 If the breast meat is one piece, cut it across into 4 slices. Flatten each by beating with a rolling pin between greaseproof paper.

2 Put the lemon juice on a plate and turn all the escalopes in it. Season on both sides, then dip both sides in flour until evenly coated.

3 Heat the butter and oil in a large frying-pan. Fry the turkey slices for 5 minutes on each side, turning them carefully with a fish slice or tongs.

4 Pour the sherry or Marsala into the pan and allow to bubble. Sprinkle over the Parmesan, then pour in the chicken stock. Cover with a lid and leave on a low heat for 10 minutes.

Chicken with curried cream

The spicy sauce in this recipe cheers up the plain grilled chicken. Canned thick cream is suitable for the sauce—and is less expensive than fresh cream—the spices provide such a good flavour no one will notice.

SERVES 4
⏲ **45 minutes**
4 chicken wing quarters
salt
freshly ground black pepper
25 g [1 oz] butter

For the sauce:
10 ml [2 teaspoons] curry paste
275 ml [½ pt] thick cream
5 ml [1 teaspoon] French mustard
salt

David Levin

1 Heat the grill to medium. Wipe the chicken joints, then season all over, rubbing in well with your fingers. Next, melt the butter in a small pan and brush over the joints.

Paul Williams

2 Place the chicken skin-side down on the grid and cook 12.5 cm [5"] away from the heat for 15 minutes. Turn and baste with more melted butter.

3 Cook for a further 20 minutes, depending on size. Check by piercing with a skewer that the chicken is cooked. If the juice runs pink, cook a further few minutes until the juice runs clear.

4 Combine all the ingredients for the sauce in a small pan and gently heat through. Transfer the chicken to a warm serving dish, pour over the sauce and serve.

---

5 Remove the turkey slices with a slotted spoon, place on a serving dish and keep warm. Spoon the juices over the turkey escalopes and serve immediately.

Chicken in spicy tomato sauce

Fried chicken is always a family favourite. Here it is finished in a sauce which also ensures that the chicken is cooked in 'awkward' places—under the wing joints, for instance—which never touch the pan base.

SERVES 4
⏲ **40 minutes**
4 chicken wing quarters
salt
freshly ground black pepper
50 g [2 oz] butter
20 ml [4 teaspoons] oil
1 small onion
30 ml [2 tablespoons] flour
2.5 ml [½ teaspoon] mustard powder
225 g [½ lb] canned tomatoes
30 ml [2 tablespoons] wine vinegar
10 ml [2 teaspoons] soft brown sugar
30 ml [2 tablespoons] tomato ketchup
25 g [1 oz] sultanas

This is a variation of the classic Cumberland sauce said to have been named after the Duke of Cumberland.

1 Rub salt and pepper into the chicken skins with your fingers.

2 Choose a large, flameproof casserole or saucepan in which the chicken joints will fit in a single layer.

3 Put the butter and oil in this and melt over a low heat. Add the chicken, skin-side down, and fry gently for 10 minutes.

4 Turn the chicken. Peel and chop the onion then sprinkle between the joints and fry for a further 5 minutes.

5 Put the flour and mustard powder into a small bowl. Add 30–45 ml [2–3 tablespoons] of the juice from the tomatoes and mix to a smooth paste. Add to the pan together with the tomatoes and their remaining juice, the vinegar, sugar, tomato ketchup and sultanas. Mix well with a wooden spoon.

6 Bring to the boil, then cover and simmer for 20 minutes. Serve immediately.

Devilled chicken with rice

Devilling was a Victorian trick—adding a sauce hot as the devil—to cheer up plain meat.

SERVES 4

⏳ **30 minutes**

8 chicken drumsticks
75 g [3 oz] margarine
15 ml [1 tablespoon] tomato purée
1 garlic clove
salt
15 ml [1 tablespoon] red wine vinegar
5 ml [1 teaspoon] prepared mustard
2.5 ml [½ teaspoon] black pepper
2.5 ml [½ teaspoon] paprika
pinch of cayenne
225 g [½ lb] long-grain rice

1 Put the margarine in a bowl with the tomato purée and mash with a fork until soft.

2 Peel and chop the garlic, then crush with salt until it makes a smooth paste. Add to the soft margarine together with the vinegar, mustard, pepper, paprika and cayenne. Beat together until well blended.

3 Heat the grill to medium and choose a gratin dish in which all the drumsticks will fit in a single layer.

4 Arrange the drumsticks in the dish, pricking the skin of the chicken in one or two places as you do so.

Paul Williams

5 Spoon or spread the devil mixture over the drumsticks and place under the grill about 12.5 cm [5"] beneath the heat for 12 minutes.

6 Put the rice in a saucepan with 575 ml [1 pt] water and 5 ml [1 teaspoon] salt. Stir once and bring to the boil. Reduce heat to simmer-point, cover and cook for 15 minutes.

7 Turn the drumsticks with tongs and baste with the sauce. Cook for a further 2 minutes.

8 Drain the cooked rice (if necessary) then fluff with a fork.

9 Check that the drumsticks are cooked through by piercing with a skewer. If the juice runs pink, cook for a further few minutes or until the juice runs clear.

10 Transfer the cooked drumsticks to a heated plate. Turn the rice into the gratin dish and stir until coated with the sauce. Arrange the drumsticks on top of the rice and serve.

Honey and pineapple gammon

Bacon chops can be used instead of gammon steak for this dish.

SERVES 4

⏳ **25 minutes**

4 gammon steaks
225 g [½ lb] 4-ring can of pineapple
30 ml [2 tablespoons] clear honey
15 ml [1 tablespoon] French mustard

1 Remove the rind from the meat. Arrange the gammon steaks or bacon chops in a flameproof dish. Heat the grill to medium.

2 Drain the juice from the pineapple rings. Reserve the rings and combine the juice with the honey and mustard.

3 Pour over the meat. Grill the meat for 15 minutes, turning at half time and basting regularly. Garnish with the pineapple rings and heat these through briefly under the grill. Serve with grilled tomato halves. Garnish with watercress.

Liver and mushroom sauté

Liver is at its best cooked only briefly; cooked for too long it becomes leathery and unappetizing. This dish takes only a few minutes to cook, leaving the liver deliciously soft and juicy.

SERVES 4
⏳ **10–15 minutes**
450 g [1 lb] lambs' or calves' liver, very thinly sliced
100 g [¼ lb] button mushrooms
100 g [¼ lb] butter
juice of a lemon
1 garlic clove
freshly chopped parsley to garnish

1 Make sure that the liver is thinly sliced. Trim away any tubes.

2 Wipe and slice the mushrooms.

3 Melt half the butter in a heavy-based frying-pan. Fry the liver for 2 minutes on each side. Lift out of the pan and keep hot.

Two really attractive dishes to give your family. Far left: honey and pineapple gammon. Below: savoury kidney supper.

4 Add the remaining butter. Add the mushrooms with the lemon juice. Peel and crush the garlic, with a little salt, and add. Sauté for about 1 minute.

5 Pour the mushrooms and buttery sauce over the liver. Sprinkle with freshly chopped parsley. Serve hot.

Savoury kidney supper

Lambs' kidneys are best for this dish as they have the finest flavour. To make the dish look really pretty use cutters to make attractive shapes for croûtes.

SERVES 4
⏳ **20 minutes**
6 lambs' kidneys
25 g [1 oz] seasoned flour
1 onion
25 g [1 oz] butter
50 g [2 oz] button mushrooms
15 ml [1 tablespoon] tomato purée
30 ml [2 tablespoons] sherry
150 ml [¼ pt] beef stock
2 thick slices of white bread
chopped parsley to garnish

1 Skin and core the kidneys and cut into thin slices. Toss the kidneys in the seasoned flour.

2 Peel and chop the onion. Sauté lightly in the butter in a frying-pan. Wipe and slice the mushrooms and add to the pan with the kidneys.

3 Combine the tomato purée, sherry and stock. Stir into the pan. Simmer for 10 minutes.

4 Toast the bread. Pile the kidney mixture into a dish. Cut toast into shapes and arrange around the edge. Garnish with the chopped parsley.

FAST FISH

Fish is often neglected by cooks for no apparent reason. In fact, there is nothing tastier than cooked fresh fish. It has all the essential nutrients one needs, being full of protein, plus the added bonus of a low-fat content. It is also a boon to the cook in a hurry because it requires little or no preparation and cooks very quickly. Most methods of cooking are both suitable and fast for fish. Grilling, frying, baking, steaming and poaching take from 10–40 minutes, depending on the type and size of the fish and whether whole, in cutlets or filleted.

Stuffed cod steaks

White fish takes very little time to prepare and can be cooked in the oven in under 30 minutes.

SERVES 4
⏳40 minutes
4 cod steaks
100 g [¼ lb] cooked ham
40 g [1½ oz] butter
1 small onion
2 medium-sized tomatoes
salt
freshly ground black pepper
50 g [2 oz] fresh white
   breadcrumbs
30–45 ml [2–3 tablespoons]
   milk

1 Heat the oven to 180°C [350°F] gas mark 4. Use 15 g [½ oz] of the butter to grease a gratin dish. Remove the central bones from the cod.

2 Dice the cooked ham. Peel and chop the onion. Sauté both gently in the remaining butter for about 5 minutes.

3 Dip the tomatoes in boiling water for 1 minute. Skin, de-seed and chop the tomatoes. Add the tomato flesh to the mixture with seasoning. Sauté for 2 minutes then remove from the heat. Stir in the breadcrumbs.

4 Stir in sufficient milk to bind the mixture. Stuff the centre of the cod steaks with the mixture and pile the remainder on top. Bake for 20–25 minutes depending on size.

Fish and cider casserole

Fish casseroles, unlike those made with meat, are quick to cook.

SERVES 4
⏳30 minutes
450 g [1 lb] cod or haddock
   fillets
2 medium-sized onions
225 g [½ lb] canned tomatoes
100 g [¼ lb] button mushrooms
275 ml [½ pt] dry cider
pinch of dried mixed herbs
salt
freshly ground black pepper
75 g [3 oz] fresh white
   breadcrumbs

1 Cut the fish into chunks and put in a casserole dish. Peel and chop the onions. Add to the flameproof casserole.

2 Add the tomatoes. Wipe and slice the mushrooms and add. Add cider and herbs and season to taste.

3 Cover the casserole and simmer over a low heat for 20 minutes. Remove from the heat.

4 Sprinkle with the breadcrumbs. Brown under a hot grill for a few minutes and serve.

Variation
●Instead of the breadcrumbs try a different topping. Mix 25 g [1 oz] grated Cheddar cheese with 50 g [2 oz] crushed potato crisps and sprinkle over the dish when it is removed from the heat. Put under a hot grill until the cheese is golden and bubbling and serve immediately

Tuna fish with eggs

Although the result is similar to baked eggs, this dish is cooked on top of the stove. It is suitable for lunch or supper but can be made more substantial; either use the same amount of tuna and a really large pan to hold twice the number of eggs, or double the amount of tuna. The olives and the tuna provide a slightly salty base that contrasts well with eggs.

SERVES 4
⏳25 minutes
4 medium-sized eggs
200 g [7 oz] canned tuna
60 ml [4 tablespoons] olive oil
2 large onions
1 garlic clove
16 green olives, stoned
large pinch cayenne pepper
15 ml [1 tablespoon] freshly
   chopped parsley
salt
freshly ground black pepper

1 Heat the oil in a frying-pan over a low heat. Peel and thinly slice the onions. Peel and chop the garlic. Add the onions and the garlic to the pan and cook until soft.

2 Meanwhile, drain then flake the tuna fish; quarter the olives.

3 Add the tuna fish, olives, cayenne pepper and parsley to the pan. Heat through.

Paul Williams

4 Using the back of a tablespoon make four depressions in the mixture. Break an egg into each depression, season lightly with salt and pepper.

5 Cover the pan and keep it over a low heat for 10 minutes until the eggs are just set. Serve straight from the pan.

Plaice with orange

Although lemon is the usual accompaniment to plaice, orange goes just as well and gives an unusual touch.

SERVES 4

⏳15 minutes

4 cross-cut plaice fillets
seasoned flour
50 g [2 oz] butter
1 small orange
15 ml [1 tablespoon] medium dry sherry
5 ml [1 teaspoon] tarragon vinegar
salt
freshly ground black pepper

1 Coat the fish in the seasoned flour. Melt all but 15 g [½ oz] of the butter in a large, heavy-based frying-pan and cook the fish for 4 minutes on each side. Lift out and keep warm.

2 Cut the orange into slices. Add the remaining butter to the pan. Add the orange, sherry, vinegar and seasoning.

3 Cook for 2 minutes. Lift out the orange slices and arrange on the fish. Pour over the sauce.

Smoked haddock gratin

Boil-in-the-bag fish is easy and clean to cook—and can be prepared from frozen, saving time. The fish and cheese go well together.

SERVES 4

⏳25 minutes

225 g [½ lb] boil-in-the-bag smoked haddock or cod
4 large eggs
25 g [1 oz] butter
25 g [1 oz] flour
275 ml [½ pt] milk
100 g [¼ lb] Cheddar cheese
25 g [1 oz] fresh breadcrumbs

1 Cook the fish following the manufacturer's instructions.

2 Hard boil the eggs.

3 Meanwhile, melt the butter in a heavy-based pan. Stir in the flour and cook for 2 minutes.

4 Stir in the milk. Bring to the boil, stirring and cook for 2 minutes. Remove from the heat.

5 Stir in the cheese. Melt over a low heat. Drain the fish. Stir the juices into the sauce.

6 Flake the fish into the base of an ovenproof dish. Slice the eggs and arrange on top. Pour over the sauce.

7 Sprinkle with the breadcrumbs and brown under a hot grill for a few minutes. Serve immediately from the dish.

Paul Williams

Plaki

This well-flavoured Greek dish can be made with frozen fish. There is no need to thaw the fish first.

SERVES 4
⏳**30 minutes**
4 frozen white fish fillets
3 large onions
15 ml [1 tablespoon] oil
225 g [½ lb] canned tomatoes
1 garlic clove
salt
freshly ground black pepper
juice and grated zest of 1 lemon

To garnish:
black olives
chopped parsley

1 Heat the oven to 220°C [425°F] gas mark 7. Put the fish in the base of an ovenproof dish.

2 Peel and chop the onions. Sauté lightly in the oil. Stir in the tomatoes.

3 Peel and crush the garlic and add to the pan with the seasonings. Simmer for 2 minutes.

4 Sprinkle lemon zest and juice over the fish. Add the onion and tomato mixture.

5 Bake in the centre of the oven for 25 minutes. Just before serving, garnish with olives and parsley.

Coronation prawns

This is based on coronation chicken—a famous curried mayonnaise dish.

SERVES 4
⏳**5 minutes**
225 g [½ lb] fresh (boiled), frozen or canned prawns
150 ml [¼ pt] mayonnaise
30 ml [2 tablespoons] apple purée
2.5 ml [½ teaspoon] curry paste
15 ml [1 tablespoon] lemon juice
salt
freshly ground black pepper
100 g [¼ lb] cooked long-grain rice
shredded lettuce

To garnish:
lemon wedges
freshly chopped parsley

1 Blend together the mayonnaise, apple purée, curry paste and lemon juice. Season to taste.

2 Drain the prawns and stir into the rice. Stir in the mayonnaise mixture.

3 Serve on a bed of shredded lettuce and garnish with lemon wedges and parsley.

Smoky pasta supper

Boil-in-the-bag smoked haddock is quick and easy to cook and goes very well with pasta shells.

SERVES 4
⏳**25 minutes**
175 g [6 oz] pasta shells
salt
5 ml [1 teaspoon] oil
3 large eggs
350 g [¾ lb] boil-in-the-bag smoked haddock or kippers
25 g [1 oz] butter
25 g [1 oz] flour
275 ml [½ pt] milk
100 g [¼ lb] Cheddar cheese, grated
freshly ground black pepper
25 g [1 oz] grated Parmesan cheese

1 Bring 1.7 L [3 pt] water to the boil. Add 7.5 ml [1½ teaspoons] salt and the oil. Add the pasta shells and cook for 8–10 minutes.

2 Meanwhile hard boil the eggs.

3 Cook the fish following the manufacturer's instructions.

4 Melt the butter in a heavy-based pan. Stir in the flour. Cook for 2 minutes. Gradually incorporate the milk. Bring to the boil, then cook gently for 5 minutes, stirring constantly. Stir in the Cheddar cheese and season the sauce lightly. Remove from heat.

5 Flake the fish. Arrange in the bottom of a flameproof dish. Shell and slice the eggs. Arrange over the fish. Heat the grill.

6 Drain the pasta shells and arrange them on the eggs. Pour over the cheese sauce. Sprinkle with grated Parmesan and brown under the grill.

SPEEDY VEG

The vegetables that you use for quick cooking should be those that are easy to prepare; and the dishes should be of the kind that do not involve too many stages of cutting, chopping and cooking. The quickest ways of cooking vegetables are usually on top of the stove. They include stir-frying and braising, steaming, boiling and simmering in a little liquid. The grill can also be very handy for certain vegetables.

Runner beans with mustard and tomato

This is a delicious way of cooking runner beans and is particularly good served with grilled meat or egg and cheese dishes. Cut the runner beans into short lengths and they will be succulent and just slightly crisp.

SERVES 4
⧗30 minutes
450 g [1 lb] runner beans
5 ml [1 teaspoon] Meaux mustard
10 ml [2 teaspoons] tomato purée
60 ml [4 tablespoons] stock
salt
freshly ground black pepper

1 String the beans and cut them into 10 cm [4"] lengths. Put them in a saucepan.

2 Mix the mustard, tomato purée, stock and seasoning together and pour them over the beans. Cover the pan and cook over a moderate heat for 20 minutes, turning the beans once or twice.

Stir-braised Brussels sprouts

This method of cooking Brussels sprouts brings out a really nutty flavour. The preparation is a little longer than for boiled or steamed sprouts, but the cooking process is a very quick one.

SERVES 4
⧗20 minutes
450 g [1 lb] Brussels sprouts
45 ml [3 tablespoons] olive oil
1 garlic clove
150 ml [¼ pt] stock
30 ml [2 tablespoons] dry sherry
10 ml [2 teaspoons] soy sauce
freshly ground black pepper

1 Trim the sprouts and cut each one in half lengthways. Heat the oil in a large frying-pan over a moderate heat. Put in the sprouts and stir them around on the heat for 1 minute.

2 Peel and finely chop the garlic. Add the garlic, stock, sherry, soy sauce and seasoning and bring to the boil. Cover the pan and leave over a moderate heat for 7 minutes until cooked.

Tempting grilled mushrooms and tomatoes with olives (page 46).

Broccoli with almonds

As broccoli spears are generally quite thick, they need a little longer cooking than other frozen vegetables in a covered pan. No other liquid is necessary. Browned almonds turn frozen broccoli into a special dinner-party dish, but for everyday you can easily omit them and start with the broccoli.

SERVES 4
⧗15 minutes
25 g [1 oz] butter
500 g [18 oz] frozen broccoli spears
50 g [2 oz] flaked almonds

1 Melt the butter in a frying-pan over a high heat. Add the almonds and stir until they are evenly browned. Remove with slotted spoon and keep warm.

2 Put the frozen broccoli into the pan. Cover the pan and cook for 8 minutes, turning the broccoli once. If by the end of the cooking time there is too much moisture in the pan, take off the lid and cook until it has evaporated.

3 Scatter the almonds over the broccoli and serve immediately.

Paul Williams

Savoy cabbage with celery

All kinds of cabbage can be simmered with a little liquid and butter or oil. Again, you can flavour it with herbs or spices, or change the cooking liquid to red or white wine, stock or cider. This recipe for crinkly Savoy cabbage and celery is light and savoury and very good with rich sautées and stews.

SERVES 4
⌛ **20 minutes**
1 medium-sized Savoy cabbage
6 large celery sticks
1 large onion
25 g [1 oz] butter
150 ml [¼ pt] dry white wine
salt
freshly ground black pepper
30 ml [2 tablespoons] chopped savory or thyme

1 Remove the outer leaves from the cabbage and shred the rest. Wash, trim and chop the celery. Peel and thinly slice the onion.

2 Put the butter and wine into a saucepan and place over a moderate heat. When the butter has melted, stir in the prepared vegetables, seasoning and herbs.

3 Cover the saucepan and cook over moderate heat for 15 minutes, stirring occasionally.

Primo cabbage with mint and yoghurt

Summer cabbage is light textured and flavoured and need only be cooked in a little oil. It will be glossy and translucent and just tender. The mint and yoghurt make it into a very summery-flavoured dish.

SERVES 4
⌛ **25 minutes**
1 medium-sized Primo (or other summer) cabbage
1 garlic clove
60 ml [4 tablespoons] olive oil
30 ml [2 tablespoons] chopped mint
salt
freshly ground black pepper
150 ml [¼ pt] natural yoghurt

1 Cut cabbage in half and finely shred. Remove the tough stalks. Peel and finely chop the garlic.

Heat the oil in a saucepan over a high heat.

2 Mix in the cabbage, garlic, mint and seasoning and stir them for 1 minute. Lower the heat, cover and cook gently for 10 minutes.

3 Remove the pan from the heat and cool the cabbage for about 30 seconds. Stir in the yoghurt, cover the pan and let the cabbage rest for 1 minute before serving.

Carrots with marjoram

Herbs and savoury mustards really improve the flavour of large carrots. When you are preparing them for cooking, simply scrub them with a stiff brush. There is no need to peel or scrape them.

SERVES 4
⌛ **30 minutes**
450 g [1 lb] carrots
25 g [1 oz] butter
150 ml [¼ pt] stock
15 ml [1 tablespoon] chopped marjoram
5 ml [1 teaspoon] Meaux mustard
salt
freshly ground black pepper

1 Slice the carrots into 6 mm [¼"] rounds. Put them into a saucepan with the rest of the ingredients and place over a moderate heat.

2 Cover and simmer for 20 minutes. Serve immediately.

Paul Williams

44

Baby carrots and currants

New baby carrots in bunches cook slightly quicker than large ones and an added advantage is that they can be cooked whole, which cuts down slightly on the preparation time. Again, just scrub them before cooking. Plumped currants and a tomato glaze turn them into a really special dish.

SERVES 4
⏳25 minutes
450 g [1 lb] baby carrots
  (or 1 bunch)
8 small spring onions
150 ml [¼ pt] stock
15 ml [1 tablespoon] tomato
  purée
30 ml [2 tablespoons] currants
salt
freshly ground black pepper

1 Scrub and trim the carrots and put them into a saucepan. Finely chop the onions.

2 Add the remaining ingredients to the pan, cover and simmer for 15 minutes. Serve.

Clockwise from front: Baby carrots and currants, Chinese cabbage and beansprouts and cauliflower with pickled cucumbers.

Cauliflower with pickled cucumbers

Quickly steamed or boiled vegetables can be finished off and made more special with melted or browned butter. The pickles in this recipe make a nice contrast to the creamy-coated cauliflower.

SERVES 4
⏳30 minutes
1 medium-sized cauliflower
1 bay leaf
2 large pickled dill cucumbers
50 g [2 oz] butter
juice or half a lemon
salt
freshly ground black pepper

1 Break the cauliflower into florets and steam them with the bay leaf for 15 minutes.

2 While the cauliflower is cooking, finely chop the cucumbers. Melt the butter in a saucepan over a high heat. When it begins to brown, stir in the lemon juice and cucumbers. Season.

3 Stir in the cauliflower, making sure all the pieces become well coated in the sauce. Transfer to a warm serving dish.

Chinese cabbage and beansprouts

For this recipe, use mung beansprouts that you have grown yourself or have bought fresh. You can also use canned ones if you drain them well first. Stir-frying makes Chinese cabbage a bright, glossy, translucent green and brings out the delicate, slightly sweet flavour.

SERVES 4
⏳10 minutes
half a large Chinese cabbage
1 large garlic clove
60 ml [4 tablespoons]
  groundnut oil
100 g [¼ lb] sprouted
  beansprouts
freshly ground black pepper
45 ml [3 tablespoons] soy
  sauce

1 Shred the Chinese cabbage. Peel and finely chop the garlic.

2 Heat the oil and garlic in a frying-pan over a high heat. Mix in the cabbage, beansprouts and seasoning and stir them around on the heat for 2 minutes.

3 Pour in the soy sauce, let it bubble and take the pan from the heat. Serve as soon as possible.

Grated courgettes with lemon

Young, fresh, fairly small courgettes are best for this recipe. Although grated, the quick cooking preserves a good, firm texture.

SERVES 4
⏳15 minutes
450 g [1 lb] courgettes
25 g [1 oz] butter
30 ml [2 tablespoons] chopped
  parsley
juice of one lemon
salt
freshly ground black pepper

1 Wipe and coarsely grate the courgettes.

2 Melt the butter in a heavy-based saucepan over a moderate heat. Stir in the courgettes, parsley, lemon juice and seasoning.

3 Cover, lower the heat and cook for 4 minutes. Serve immediately while they are fresh and white.

Cucumber with fennel and lemon

This vegetable goes very well with fish, or as a complete contrast with richly-sauced meat dishes. The cucumber should be slightly crisp when cooked—it will have a pleasant but sharp taste, so portions are small.

SERVES 4.
⏳ **20 minutes**
1 small cucumber
15 g [½ oz] butter
juice of half a lemon
30 ml [2 tablespoons] chopped Florentine fennel
salt
freshly ground black pepper

1 Chop the cucumber into 12 mm [½"] dice.

2 Put it into a saucepan with the butter, lemon juice, fennel and seasoning. Cover and place over a low heat for 15 minutes, stirring occasionally.

Honey-glazed peas and carrots

This recipe combines both canned and frozen vegetables. The honey gives them an attractive glaze and slightly sweet flavour.

SERVES 4
⏳ **15 minutes**
500 g [18 oz] canned carrots
275 g [10 oz] frozen petits pois
5 ml [1 teaspoon] honey
15–30 ml [1–2 tablespoons] chopped parsley

1 Drain the carrots, reserving 150 ml [¼ pt] of the liquid. Pour this liquid into a saucepan and bring to the boil.

2 Add the peas and honey and bring to the boil again. Add the carrots and boil rapidly, uncovered, until all the moisture has evaporated and the carrots and peas are attractively glazed.

3 Stir in the parsley and serve immediately.

Stir-fried marrow with salami

If marrow is plainly simmered or steamed, it can be quite tasteless and uninteresting. Stir-frying is an ideal method to use as the quick heat drives off moisture and the slices of marrow become a bright green. The browned garlic gives the marrow a nutty flavour and the salami makes the dish a sub-stantial one. Serve with cold meats.

SERVES 4
⏳ **20 minutes**
1 small marrow
100 g [¼ lb] salami
1 small onion
1 small garlic clove
60 ml [4 tablespoons] olive oil
15 ml [1 tablespoon] chopped thyme
salt
freshly ground black pepper
45 ml [3 tablespoons] white wine vinegar

1 Cut the marrow in half, scoop out the seeds and discard. Peel the marrow, cut each half lengthways and slice the quarters thinly across. Skin and cut each slice of salami into quarters. Peel and thinly slice the onion. Peel and finely chop the garlic.

2 Heat the oil in a frying-pan over a high heat. Mix in the marrow, salami, onion and garlic. Fry them for 2 minutes, moving them about in the pan continually with a fork.

3 Add the thyme and seasoning. Pour in the vinegar and let it bubble. Serve immediately.

Mushrooms and tomatoes with olives

Mushrooms can be brushed with melted butter or olive oil and plainly grilled; or they can be topped with something bright and tasty. These go well with lamb or beef.

SERVES 4
⏳ **20 minutes**
12 large, flat mushrooms, stalks removed
25 g [1 oz] butter, melted
approximately 10 ml [2 teaspoons] French mustard
4 large firm tomatoes
salt
freshly ground black pepper
6 black olives

1 Brush the mushrooms with the melted butter and place on a heat-proof serving plate, black side up.

2 Spread them very thinly with the mustard.

3 Cut each tomato into 3 thick slices. Season lightly.

4 Using a cherry stoner, remove the olive stones or halve the olives with a knife.

5 Heat the grill to high and grill the mushrooms for 2 minutes, or until they are just cooked through.

6 Put a slice of tomato on each mushroom. Top with an olive half.

7 Return the mushrooms to the grill until the tomatoes are really hot and the olives sizzling.

Leeks with tarragon

If leeks are sliced quite thinly they can be cooked very quickly. Even if you are in a hurry, always make sure that you wash them properly under running water before cooking, otherwise they could be gritty and unpleasant. Tarragon and tarragon vinegar give them an unusual sweet-sharp flavour that is excellent with pork or lamb.

SERVES 4
⧗ **20 minutes**
450 g [1 lb] leeks
25 g [1 oz] butter
5 ml [1 teaspoon] dried tarragon
75 ml [5 tablespoons] stock
15 ml [1 tablespoon] tarragon vinegar

Paul Williams

1 Trim, wash then slice the leeks into 6 mm [¼″] rounds. Rinse again. Melt butter in a pan over a low heat. Stir in the leeks and dried tarragon.

2 When the leeks are well-coated with butter, stir in the stock and tarragon vinegar. Cover and cook gently for 10 minutes.

Simmered tomatoes with basil ✓

Once you have peeled the tomatoes for this recipe, the cooking method is very simple and quick. The basil is important if the dish is to be really effective—it always gives tomatoes a special flavour. If you do have not any fresh, use 15 ml [1 tablespoon] dried basil and mix this into the butter before you add the tomatoes.

SERVES 4
⧗ **20 minutes**
700 g [1½ lb] small, firm tomatoes
1 garlic clove
25 g [1 oz] butter
30 ml [2 tablespoons] chopped fresh basil

1 Dip the tomatoes into boiling water for 1 minute. Remove with a perforated spoon and skin them. Peel and finely chop the garlic.

2 Melt the butter in a heavy-based saucepan over a low heat. Add the garlic and the whole tomatoes. Turn them in the butter to coat them all over.

3 Scatter the basil over the top, cover and cook gently for 5 minutes, turning occasionally, so that the tomatoes heat through but stay firm.

Two quick and tasty vegetables dishes— distinctive-flavoured leeks with tarragon and sweet-tasting honey-glazed peas and carrots. Both make excellent accompaniments to hot or cold pork and lamb dishes.

Paul Williams

SUPER SALADS

Salads made from fresh, raw vegetables are quick to prepare and an excellent source of vitamins. Freshness is essential and you must aim for variety if you make them regularly. It is a good idea to make mayonnaise and French dressing in quantity if you eat several salads in a week. Covered with cling film, mayonnaise will keep in the refrigerator for as long as two weeks. French dressing will keep in a cool cupboard for about three weeks.

Colourful cabbage, grape and satsuma salad.

With ready-prepared dressings, all you have to do is to slice up the vegetables and add a little garlic or a flavouring such as Meaux, a spicy granular mustard, when the time comes to make the salad. If you buy mayonnaise, make sure it contains real egg yolk and is not a 'salad cream'.

Vinaigrette

This classic French dressing turns an assortment of cold (and sometimes hot) vegetables, both raw and cooked, into an interesting and tasty dish. Make up the dressing in large amounts, as given, and store in a screw-top jar in a cool cupboard.

MAKES 250 ML [9 FL OZ]
1 minute
75 ml [3 fl oz] wine vinegar
salt
freshly ground black pepper
175 ml [6 fl oz] olive oil

1 Measure the wine vinegar into a bowl or jug. Add salt and pepper to taste and stir with a fork.

2 Pour on the oil and beat vigorously with a fork to mix and thicken.

Variations
Change the flavourings to suit the salad. If you are serving identical ingredients on two successive nights, change the dressing to add variety. Add any of the following to 90 ml [6 tablespoons] dressing:
● 1 garlic clove, crushed with salt.
● 10 ml [2 teaspoons] made mustard.
● pinch of paprika, cayenne or cinnamon.
● dash of sauce, such as soy, anchovy essence, Worcestershire or Tabasco.
● 30 ml [2 tablespoons] freshly chopped herbs: choose from chives, parsley, tarragon, basil and marjoram.
● 10 ml [2 teaspoons] dried mixed herbs.
● 5 ml [1 teaspoon] sugar.

Paul Williams

Mayonnaise

Delicious with cold chicken and fish, mayonnaise will also transform uninspiring odds and ends like left-over cooked vegetables into a real salad. Make sure all the ingredients are at room temperature as this helps to prevent curdling.

MAKES 300 ML [11 FL OZ]
⏳ **10 minutes**
2 large eggs yolks
2.5 ml [½ teaspoon] made mustard
pinch of salt
15 ml [1 tablespoon] wine vinegar or lemon juice
275 ml [½ pt] olive oil, or a mixture of half olive oil/ half corn oil

1 Warm a bowl in hot water and dry it very carefully. Stand it on a cloth.

2 Put the mustard in the bottom of the bowl then stir in the egg yolks. Beat for 1–2 minutes until the yolks are thick and sticky. Add the salt and vinegar or lemon juice and beat again for half a minute.

3 Add 2 drops of oil and beat round the sides and base of the bowl until the oil is completely incorporated. When it is absorbed add another 2 drops. Never stop beating: change hands if necessary.

4 Add a scant 5 ml [1 teaspoon] of oil and continue beating. As the mixture thickens, you can add the oil a little more generously. When all the oil is used, check the seasonings.

5 To ensure the mayonnaise will keep, beat in 15–30 ml [1–2 tablespoons] boiling water. Cover the bowl with cling film and store in the refrigerator.

Quick sour cream dressing

This dressing has a thick, creamy consistency, similar to mayonnaise, but is much quicker to make. It is particularly good with hot vegetables.

MAKES 150 ML [¼ PT]
⏳ **1 minute**
1 small garlic clove
salt
150 ml [¼ pt] soured cream
15 ml [1 tablespoon] lemon juice
freshly ground black pepper

1 Peel, then chop the garlic and crush with a little salt.

2 Add to the soured cream together with the lemon juice and a good shake of black pepper. Blend together then check seasonings.

Cabbage, grape and satsuma salad

Fruity and refreshing flavours are added to this white cabbage salad.

SERVES 4
⏳ **20 minutes**
half a small white cabbage
100 g [¼ lb] green grapes
4 satsumas
50 g [2 oz] raisins
1 garlic clove (optional)
salt
60 ml [4 tablespoons] olive oil
30 ml [2 tablespoons] white wine vinegar
freshly ground black pepper

1 Shred the cabbage. Halve and deseed the grapes. Peel the satsumas and pull them into segments. Place in a salad bowl with the raisins.

2 Peel, then crush the garlic (if used) with a little salt, pressing it with a round-bladed knife.

3 Beat the remaining ingredients together to make the dressing, add the garlic and fold into the salad.

Pineapple and cress salad

Fresh pineapple makes a refreshing, luxury salad. If you have not any fresh coriander, use chervil or parsley. Increase or decrease the amount to taste.

SERVES 4
⏳ **15 minutes**
half a fresh pineapple
1 bunch watercress
1 carton mustard and cress
15 ml [1 tablespoon] chopped fresh coriander
2.5 ml [½ teaspoon] ground coriander
1 garlic clove (optional)
salt
60 ml [4 tablespoons] olive oil
zest and juice of half a large orange

1 Dice the pineapple and chop the watercress, removing thick stalks and yellow leaves. Put them into a salad bowl. Cut up the mustard and cress and add. Add the fresh coriander.

2 To make the dressing, put the ground coriander and peeled garlic, crushed with a little salt, if using, into a bowl. Beat in the oil and orange juice. Mix in the orange zest and fold the dressing into the salad.

Variation
● Use 3 large oranges instead of the pineapple and substitute the zest and juice of 1 lemon for the half orange in the dressing.

Paul Williams

Spicy sweetcorn salad

This is a tasty and substantial salad, using quick canned sweetcorn. Softening the onions first gives them a very mellow flavour—they would be too strong if used raw.

SERVES 4
⏳ 15 minutes
350 g [¾ lb] canned
   sweetcorn
1 large onion
1 large garlic clove
60 ml [4 tablespoons] olive oil
1 large green pepper
5 ml [1 teaspoon] paprika
5 ml [1 teaspoon] Tabasco
   sauce
30 ml [2 tablespoons] white
   wine vinegar
salt
freshly ground black pepper
225 g [½ lb] tomatoes

1 Drain the sweetcorn. Peel and finely chop the onion and garlic. Put the oil in a saucepan over a low heat, add the onion and garlic. Cook them until they are transparent and are just beginning to soften.

2 Core, de-seed and finely chop the pepper. Mix the pepper, paprika, corn, Tabasco and vinegar into the onions. Season to taste with salt and pepper.

3 Take the pan from the heat and transfer everything to a salad bowl. Cool the salad (speed this by putting it into the refrigerator for a short time).

4 Chop the tomatoes and mix them into the salad just before serving. Check seasoning.

Cress and mustard salad

Mustard and cress is one salad combination that is available all the year round. The mustard powder gives this salad a savoury taste and the seeds give an interesting spicy hotness. It is advisable to make and eat this salad on the same day.

SERVES 4
⏳ 15 minutes
6 firm medium-sized tomatoes
half a small cucumber
2 cartons mustard and cress

30 ml [2 tablespoons] olive oil
15 ml [1 tablespoons] cider
   vinegar
10 ml [2 teaspoons] mustard
   seed
5 ml [1 teaspoon] mustard
   powder
salt
freshly ground black pepper

1 Dice the tomatoes and cucumber and put them into a salad bowl. Chop the mustard and cress and add.

2 Mix the rest of the ingredients together to make the dressing and fold it into the salad. Serve immediately.

Carrot and swede salad

By changing the flavourings and dressings you can make the same vegetable appear as a totally different salad. Swedes with carrots make a savoury salad, superb with beef.

SERVES 4
⏳ 20 minutes
350 g [¾ lb] carrots
350 g [¾ lb] swedes
1 garlic clove
150 ml [¼ pt] soured cream
30 ml [2 tablespoons] white
   wine vinegar
5 ml [1 teaspoon] mustard
   powder
15 ml [1 tablespoon] grated
   horseradish
salt
freshly ground black pepper

Roger Phillips

1 Grate the carrots and swedes coarsely and place them in a salad bowl. Peel and finely chop the garlic.

2 Beat the remaining ingredients together to make the dressing. Add the garlic, then stir into the salad. Leave the salad to stand for 15 minutes before serving.

Carrot and apple salad with banana

This is a really substantial salad, ideal with cold meats or with egg dishes and quiches. Do not be frightened of the bananas—they make a thick and creamy dressing but it is not oversweet. Eat it immediately, before the bananas can discolour. Serve on a bed of watercress.

SERVES 4
⏳ 20 minutes
2 medium-sized bananas
60 ml [4 tablespoons] natural
   yoghurt
45 ml [3 tablespoons] cider
   vinegar
freshly ground black pepper
1 large garlic clove
salt
2 medium-sized tart dessert
   apples
350 g [¾ lb] carrots
100 g [¼ lb] peanuts
50 g [2 oz] sultanas

1 Peel, then mash the bananas. Blend in the yoghurt, vinegar and pepper to taste.

2 Peel and crush the garlic with salt and add. Turn the mixture into a salad bowl.

3 Peel the apples and grate them into the bananas, mixing as you go. Repeat with the carrots. Mix in the peanuts and sultanas.

Cauliflower and orange salad

Finely chopped raw cauliflower is surprisingly pleasant to eat, as it crumbles as soon as you bite it. This salad with oranges has the light sweetness of coriander in the dressing.

SERVES 4
⏳ 10 minutes
1 medium-sized cauliflower
1 large orange
1 garlic clove
salt
60 ml [4 tablespoons] olive oil
30 ml [2 tablespoons] cider
   vinegar
30 ml [2 tablespoons]
   unsweetened orange juice
5 ml [1 teaspoon] ground
   coriander
freshly ground black pepper

1 Break the cauliflower into small florets, removing any thick stalk and leaves. Then chop the florets finely. Put the cauliflower into a salad bowl.

2 Peel the orange, pull it into segments and roughly slice them. Mix the orange with the cauliflower florets.

3 Peel and crush the garlic with a little salt. Beat the rest of the ingredients together to make the dressing. Add the garlic and fold the dressing into the salad.

Mixed salad with olives

This is a bright and colourful salad with an Italian flavour.

SERVES 4
⏳ 15 minutes
1 medium-sized cabbage lettuce
  or a small cos lettuce
450 g [1 lb] firm tomatoes
1 large orange
12 green olives, stoned and quartered
1 garlic clove
salt
60 ml [4 tablespoons] olive oil
30 ml [2 tablespoons] white wine vinegar
30 ml [2 tablespoons] freshly chopped parsley, marjoram and thyme
freshly ground black pepper

1 Wash the lettuce, tear it into small pieces and put it into a salad bowl. Chop the tomatoes.

2 Remove the rind and pith from the orange, cut the segments free from the pith and quarter them.

3 Put the lettuce, tomatoes, orange and olive pieces into a salad bowl. Peel and crush the garlic with a little salt.

4 Beat the oil, vinegar, garlic, herbs and pepper together to make the dressing and pour over the salad. Toss salad in the dressing and serve immediately.

Delightful mixed salad with olives.

SWEET AND SIMPLE

Keep well-stocked with fruit. The quickest of meals—and nutritionally a good idea—is bread with a good variety of cheese, followed by fruit. Raw dessert fruit is quick to prepare and is perfect served in bowls, simply sprinkled with sugar and accompanied by pouring cream. Fruit salads can be quick to prepare; instead of making the sugar syrup in which the fruit is usually served, just stir in some clear honey or some ginger syrup from a jar of preserved ginger.

Canned fruit keep for at least a year, so that it is worth having a selection in your store cupboard. If you are keeping these for unexpected visitors, rather than the family, go for more unusual fruit like mangoes and lychees.

Many fruit can be made into delicious cooked desserts in a very short time. Fruit can be fried very quickly in butter in a shallow frying-pan and when it is a delicious golden-brown, you can add spices and sugar or another tasty sweetener, such as golden syrup. It is a good idea to prepare these dishes before you eat the main course and then quickly cook them just before serving. This way, they go direct from pan to table and have no chance to become soggy.

Grilling is another very quick, but nevertheless impressive way of cooking fruit. The fruits most often grilled are apples, bananas, pineapples and peaches. Grilling is an excellent way of making ordinary canned fruit look

like something you have planned specially. Grilled grapefruit halves are usually kept for the first course but oranges can be grilled in the same way and served as a sweet course.

Although jellies take some time to set, they can be made very quickly. To save squeezing or crushing fruit, use cans, bottles or cartons of fruit juice. Make the jellies before you start the rest of the meal, so that they can set while you finish cooking and eat the main course. Put them in individual glasses to shorten the setting time. If they still have not set, pop them in the freezer or ice compartment of the refrigerator for a few minutes.

David Levin

Gingered marmalade apples

In this recipe, soft, melting apple rings are covered with a golden sauce of bitter-sweet marmalade. To prevent the apples discolouring if you want to prepare them in advance, put a little lemon juice in a bowl and turn each apple in it. Other ground spices, such as cinnamon or mixed spice, can be used in place of ginger if preferred.

SERVES 4
⌛ 30 minutes
6 small or 4 large crisp
**   dessert apples**
40 g [1½ oz] butter
5–10 ml [1–2 teaspoons]
**   ground ginger**
60 ml [4 tablespoons] fine cut
**   orange marmalade**

1 Peel and core the apples and cut them into rounds 6 mm [¼"] thick.

2 Melt 25 g [1 oz] of the butter in a large frying-pan over a high heat. When the foam has subsided put in as many apple slices as the pan will hold in a single layer. Turn them after 2 minutes and cook for a further 2–3 minutes until coloured. Remove and keep warm.

3 Add the remaining butter to the pan if necessary and cook the remaining apple rings.

4 Lower the heat and return all the apples to the pan. Sprinkle them with ginger to taste. Spoon in the marmalade and allow it to melt over the apple rounds. Serve immediately.

Honeyed bananas with raisins

Raisins make an attractive and sweet addition to bananas in a clear honey sauce. Serve with a bowl of whipped cream or a jug of pouring cream.

SERVES 4
⌛ 30 minutes
4 firm bananas
40 g [1½ oz] butter
50 g [2 oz] raisins
45 ml [3 tablespoons] clear
**   honey**

1 Peel the bananas and cut them in half crossways. Cut each piece in half lengthways.

2 Melt 25 g [1 oz] of the butter in a large frying-pan over a high heat. When the foaming subsides, put in as many pieces of banana as the pan will hold in a single layer. Fry them 1–2 minutes then turn over. Cook a further 1–2 minutes until coloured. Remove to a warm serving dish.

3 Cook any remaining pieces in the same way using the remaining butter if necessary. Set aside with the other pieces.

4 Lower the heat and allow the pan to cool a little. Put in the raisins and cook them for 30 seconds.

5 Return all the pieces of banana to the frying-pan. Spoon in the honey and let it melt. Transfer everything to a warm serving plate.

Pineapple flamed in rum

This is a dish with which to impress guests. The gently browned pineapple rings are coated in a sticky rum glaze.

SERVES 4
⌛ 30 minutes
1 good-sized pineapple
40 g [1½ oz] butter
120 ml [8 tablespoons] dark
**   rum**
60 ml [4 tablespoons] Barbados
**   sugar**
30 ml [2 tablespoons] toasted
**   hazelnuts**

1 Cut the foliage from the top of the pineapple and a slice from the bottom with a sharp, serrated knife. Cut the husk from the pineapple. Cut the flesh into 1 cm [⅓"] slices and stamp out the cores with an apple corer.

2 Melt 25 g [1 oz] of the butter in a large frying-pan over a high heat. When the foam has subsided, put in as many pieces of pineapple as the pan will take in a single layer. Brown them on both sides. Remove and keep warm.

3 Add the remaining butter to the pan if necessary and cook the rest of the pineapple.

4 Warm the rum in a small pan over a low heat.

David Levin

5 Return all the pineapple slices to the pan and sprinkle the sugar over them.

6 Set fire to the rum, stand well back and pour it over the pineapple.

7 As soon as the flame dies, transfer the pineapple to a warm serving dish and scatter the toasted hazelnuts over the top.

Grilled peach crumble

On occasions when you do not have any fresh fruit, canned peaches can be given a lift out of the ordinary by heating them. A simple mixture of browned breadcrumbs, cinnamon and sugar gives them a crispy topping.

SERVES 4
⌛ 20 minutes
800 g [1¾ lb] canned peach
**   halves**
75 g [3 oz] butter
25 g [1 oz] browned
**   breadcrumbs**
5 ml [1 teaspoon] ground
**   cinnamon**
125 g [1 oz] Demerara sugar

1 Heat the grill to moderate and use 15 g [½ oz] butter to grease a heat-proof dish.

2 Drain the peach halves in a sieve over a bowl and put them in the dish, rounded side up.

3 Put the dish under the grill so that the peaches are about 5 cm [2"] away from the heat. Cook them for 2–3 minutes. Mix the breadcrumbs, cinnamon and sugar together.

4 Turn the peaches over and top them with the breadcrumb mixture. Dot them with the remaining butter.

5 Return to the grill for a further 2–3 minutes, or until the crumbs are sizzling. Serve immediately.

Pineapple in orange caramel sauce

Orange juice and Barbados sugar can be quickly made into a delicious sauce for grilled pineapple.

SERVES 4
⏳ 25 minutes
1 medium-sized pineapple
25 g [1 oz] butter
90 ml [6 tablespoons] unsweetened orange juice
40 g [1½ oz] Barbados sugar

Roger Phillips

1 Cut the foliage from the top of the pineapple and a slice from the bottom with a sharp, serrated knife. Cut the husk from the pineapple.

2 Cut the flesh into 8 slices and stamp out the cores with an apple corer.

3 Heat the grill to moderate.

4 Lay the slices of pineapple on a heatproof dish.

5 Put the butter into a saucepan and melt it over a low heat. Remove before it foams and use to brush the pineapple.

6 Put the orange juice and sugar into a saucepan and stir them together over a low heat until the sugar dissolves. Spoon the liquid over the pineapple.

7 Put the dish under the grill so the pineapple is about 5 cm [2″] away from the heat.

8 Cook for 2 minutes then turn over. Brown on the second side, cooking for 2–3 minutes.

Variation
● Substitute 30 ml [2 tablespoons] of the orange juice with rum.

Gingered bananas

Whenever you finish up a jar of preserved stem ginger, save the syrup as you will find you can use it for cooking grilled fruit or for stirring into fruit salads. It is used for these bananas and they are topped with stem ginger as well. They can be served with whipped cream or plain yoghurt.

SERVES 4
⏳ 20 minutes
4 firm bananas
4 pieces stem ginger
25 g [1 oz] butter
60 ml [4 tablespoons] syrup from preserved ginger

1 Heat the grill to high. Peel the bananas and cut them in half lengthways. Lay them in a heatproof dish. Finely chop the ginger and set aside.

2 Melt the butter in a saucepan over a low heat, but remove before it foams. Brush the butter over the bananas. Spoon the ginger syrup over the bananas.

3 Put the dish under the grill so the bananas are about 5 cm [2″] away from the heat. Cook the bananas for about 3 minutes. Turn them over and baste with the syrup. Cook for about 5 minutes until they are golden brown.

4 Scatter the chopped ginger over the top. Serve the bananas from the dish.

Apple rings with cloves and honey

Fresh fruit must be brushed before grilling with melted butter and slightly sweetened with sugar, syrup or honey as it has no sweet syrup of its own. Serve these delicious apples with whipped cream.

SERVES 4
⏳ 25 minutes
4 medium-sized cooking apples
25 g [1 oz] butter
45 ml [3 tablespoons] honey
2.5 ml [½ teaspoon] ground cloves

1 Peel and core the apples and cut them into 6 mm [¼″] thick rings.

David Levin

2 Heat the grill to high.

3 Arrange the apple rings in a large shallow heatproof dish, overlapping as little as possible. (Use two small dishes if you do not have one large enough.)

4 Melt the butter in a saucepan over a low heat, but remove from the heat before it foams. Brush the butter over the apples.

5 Put the honey into a saucepan with the cloves and melt over a low heat. Spoon over the apples.

6 Put the dish under the grill so the apple rings are about 10 cm [4″] from the heat and cook them until they are brown and bubbling—about 3 minutes. Turn and baste them and give them 4–5 minutes on the second side. Serve them straight from the dish.

Quick melon and ginger.

David Levin

Quick melon and ginger

Although melon is usually served as a first course, it can also be made into a sweet. In this recipe it is filled with a creamy ginger syllabub and topped with walnuts.

SERVES 4–6
⏳ 15 minutes
1 medium-sized honeydew
  melon
225 [¼ pt] thick cream
15 ml [1 tablespoon] syrup
  from preserved ginger
4 pieces stem ginger
50 g [2 oz] chopped walnuts

1 Cut the melon into 4–6 slices. Scoop out the seeds. Put each slice into a dish.

2 Whip the cream until it is thick enough to hold its shape and then whip in the syrup.

3 Finely chop the stem ginger and fold it into the cream. Pile the cream on the melon slices. Scatter walnuts on top.

Citrus fruit salad

Oranges, grapefruit and bananas make a bitter-sweet and refreshing salad.

SERVES 4
⏳ 20 minutes
4 medium-sized oranges
2 large grapefruit
60 ml [4 tablespoons] clear
  honey
2 bananas

1 With a sharp knife, peel the oranges and grapefruit over a plate, removing rind, pith and the fine skin of the fruit.

2 To separate the segments, cut down the side of the segment, with the knife against the skin. Then turn the knife to free the flesh. Repeat this all the way round the fruit.

3 Put the fruit in a bowl, adding juice from the plate and squeezing out the skins. Fold in the honey and chill for 10 minutes.

4 Peel and slice the bananas and fold into the fruit just before serving.

Blackcurrant cream

The whipped cream is stained an attractive light pink colour when the blackcurrants are folded into it. The blackcurrants and syrup on top make a pretty contrast in colour.

SERVES 4
⏳ 15 minutes
2 × 450 g [1 lb] canned
  blackcurrants
275 ml [½ pt] thick cream

Simple brandied cherries make a superb dinner-party dessert that will be guaranteed to impress your guests.

1 Turn the blackcurrants into a sieve over a bowl and reserve the syrup.

2 Whip the cream until it will stand in peaks when the whisk is removed. Fold in half the blackcurrants.

3 Pipe the cream into individual glass dishes and top with the remaining blackcurrants. Spoon 15 ml [1 tablespoon] syrup over each dish.

Peach and cheese biscuits

Instead of chopping peaches and mixing them into the cheese, you can pile the cheese on top of the peaches. The digestive biscuits in this recipe make the dish more interesting. Serve with a cake slice.

SERVES 4
⏲ **20 minutes**
400 [[14 oz] canned peaches
8 digestive biscuits
225 g [½ lb] Philadelphia cheese
25–40 g [1–1½ oz] caster sugar
8 walnut halves

1 Turn the peaches into a sieve over a bowl and reserve the juice.

2 Put the biscuits on to a large, flat serving plate and spoon 15 ml [1 tablespoon] of the juice over each one.

3 Put the cheese into a bowl and beat it until soft. Beat in the sugar.

4 Arrange a peach half, rounded side down, on to each biscuit.

5 Pile the cheese on to the peach halves and top each with a walnut half.

6 Leave for 15 minutes before serving so the biscuits have a chance to soften.

Brandied cherries

The longer you can leave the cherries in the brandy before serving, the better. Make this sweet before you begin the preceding courses of the meal.

SERVES 4
⏲ **35 minutes**
2 × 425 g [15 oz] canned black cherries
150 ml [¼ pt] brandy
toasted flaked almonds

1 Drain the black cherries.

2 Put the cherries into a bowl. Pour the brandy over them and leave to macerate for at least 30 minutes.

3 Put in individual dishes. Scatter over the almonds just before serving.

INDEX